Short Summer in South America

Nick Sanders

ASHFORD
Southampton

Published by Ashford,
1 Church Road, Shedfield, Hampshire SO3 2HW

British Library Cataloguing in Publication Data
Sanders, Nick, *1957*–
Short summer in South America.
1. South America. Description and travel
I. Title
918'.0438

ISBN 1–85253–201–7

Printed in Great Britain by
Hartnolls Limited, Bodmin, Cornwall, England
Phototypeset in 11/12pt Palatino by Input Typesetting Ltd., London

The author and publisher thank the Estate of Pablo Neruda, Nathaniel Tarn
(translator) and Jonathan Cape Ltd, for granting permission to reprint the extract
quoted on p. 119; and Martin Secker & Warburg Limited for granting permission
to reprint the extract quoted on p. 138.

ACKNOWLEDGEMENTS

With thanks to: Steve Bell and Steve Parker at Raleigh
Bicycles; to Tommy Dick and family in Punta Arenas; to
the Bridges-Goodhall family in Viamonte; to the Gonzales
family in Gaiman; to Enrique Guiza and family in Arica; to
Graham and Martha in Lima.
Also thanks to Hugh Joseph for editing the manuscript com-
passionately! And a very, very special thanks to Mr Bob Lyall
in Santiago.

For
Linda

ILLUSTRATIONS

PROLOGUE

It was 8.30pm and still the sun had not set. England was in the grip of a limp, moist winter and I had suddenly switched to summer on the other side of the world. The curtains of the carriage windows fluttered in a late-evening breeze that had crept along the length of the train. A portly waiter, with the dazed eyes of one press-ganged into service, was asking each passenger if he or she should like to dine at the first or second sitting. As he wrote out the appropriate ticket, strands of oily hair slopped forward over his eyes only to be pushed back by pudgy fingers. Each ticket bore the imprint of his fingers. The waiter rocked in the central aisle as if he were sailing around Cape Horn. He had probably journeyed on this route for longer than he could remember, and only holidays, breakdowns, earthquakes, coups, wives and mistresses would have stopped him from going to where this railway meets the sea. Yellow fields of rape flashed past the windows of the carriage, alternating with stripes of lavender in between valleys carpeted with vines. It was time for dinner. Gripping the head of each seat, so as not to be thrown, crashing, into the arms of the waiters, I made for the dining car.

The waiters in the dining car had the air of men whose youth had given way to an easy middle age; indeed, their expressions suggested that the excitement of rushing through one of the world's most beautiful and fruitful valleys had long been replaced by a level expectation of nothing. Few can travel more than these men. Most of their lives they eat, sleep, think, move and dream at 50mph. Only the station halts allow for an uninterrupted lungful of air before the train's forward motion is heralded by a charge of clanging carriages.

So, once again, they hurtle through the heartland of Chile, a country whose geography consists of a massive north–south valley, the eastern half supporting the Andes mountain chain, the western slopes descending to the wave-pounding Pacific.

The names of the trains seem to offer you an adventure; the *Rapido del Calle Calle*, daily to Valdivia; the *Osorno Rapido* and trains to Rancagua, Curico, Talca, Chillan, Pichilemu, Puerto Varas and Puerto Montt. But, looking into the eyes of the waiters, I saw reflected the fear of the traveller: that magnificence can become tempered by routine and a certain weariness; that, like driftwood, consciousness can be dispersed and deadened by the dreary routine of a static way of life.

It was a struggle to summon up the courage to pay a dollar for a *pisco* sour, a quarter of a day's budget on a single drink. The pisco was as sharp as it was cool and as earthy as the ground from which it was squeezed. An old waiter stood by the bar, stooped and gnarled. He brought me a second drink on a silver tray. The restaurant was empty except for two heavily accented Americans who sat facing me on a separate table. 'We were just talking statistics,' one of them said, encouraging me to join in their conversation. 'By the year 2000 half the population of the USA will be Hispanic.'

'We're just *scarcing* ourselves out of existence,' the other said, drawling noisily around his pipe. Both had large heads, and padded cheeks that filled out face lines and made me think of a baby.

'More water, *por favor*,' said the pipe smoker to the waiter, before introducing himself to me as Father Leo. 'We're both priests from Chicago but we had parishes in the south of here for twenty-seven years. We've come back for a holiday.'

For thirty years they had been part of the Precious Blood Brotherhood, a name that conjured up more than a hint of ritual.

'I knew a priest, Brother Elliot, who worked for the Sacred Heart of Jesus in Uganda and he came from Louisiana,' I said.

'Sure thing, we're all over the place,' said Father Leo, his face spreading wide as he smiled.

'We were just saying,' the other priest said, looking like a middle-aged Olive Oil with a plaster strapped over a sunburnt nose, 'you don't get the blacks using birth control. Economic circumstances and bias create poverty with children that cannot be afforded.'

'Ah, but do you put a price on the love of a child?' Father Leo asked, turning to his colleague.

'I wonder if you can, Father. They say that one in three people know someone with AIDS. But I ask you, do you know anyone?' Father Leo fingered his cup and tensed visibly.

'Everybody in San Francisco probably knows three people who've got it, so what does that prove about statistics?'

At the time I had never heard of AIDS and, feeling myself progressively out of depth as the conversation developed, I changed the subject:

'Do you think my morality could be questioned by journeying in a country ruled by a military dictatorship?' Father Leo said that was difficult to answer and he would have to think about it. I too wondered about the travellers who walk and run, bus or cycle their way along the mighty Andes. Already, there was a team of cyclists riding down from Alaska towards the southern end of the Pan American Highway. Yet against the prevailing wind, they will battle so hard. A wind that will absorb all reasons for the journey other than the physical process needed to survive. Around the time I leave the train, they will set out on a 12,000 mile route where 20 per cent of their available awareness will be dissipated into the wind.

'They do say that a people gets the government it deserves,' Father Leo continued. 'In the US, we have a president that says either "You're on my side" or "You're a Commie", so I suppose that makes me a Commie,' he laughed. 'It's just that our regime is more polished, more refined. And here, well, agriculture is stable; the *peso* is stable. Allende didn't solve the problems. Only 30 per cent of the population voted for him and the rest of the vote was split with thirty opposition parties, so he got in.'

Because I liked the name, I had intended to get off the train at a small town called Frutilla. There, the journey would begin. But, at this small South American station deep in Chile, the train arrived, paused and passed. The carriage door had become jammed and with a feeling of doom I tried in vain to alight. The next stop was Puerto Varas, I could always try there. Throwing everything on to the platform, I bundled myself together to start the journey. The first turn of the pedal was about to launch me into an adventure that would weave through the Antarctic archipelago, cross the Straits of Magellan, battle into a Patagonian headwind and swelter in the Atacama desert . . .

Caracas
VENEZUELA
•Bogota
COLOMBIA
Quito•
Ecuador
Cuenca
Piura
PERU
Trujillo
Lima
Ica
Nazca
Cuzco
Puno
BOLIVIA
La Paz
Tacna
Arica
Angofasia
Calama
PARAGUAY
Copiapo
CHILE
Coquimbo
ARGENTINA
SOUTH PACIFIC
OCEAN
Mendoza
Santiago
Curico
Buenos
Aires
URAGUAY
Los Angeles
SOUTH ATLANTIC
OCEAN
Puerto de Valdivia
River
Chubut
Puerto Montt
Trelew
Esquel
Paso de Indios
Las Plumas
Comodoro Rivadavia
Santa Cruz
Punta Arenas
Porvenir
San Sebastián
Ushuaia

BRAZIL

Brasilia

Route taken by author
through South America

ONE

As I turned right out of the station I could already feel the tranquillity of this little German town. The road was pieced together in fawn-coloured concrete slabs, a thin sandwich of black tarmac glueing them together. I turned left down a hill and freewheeled into the town centre. Outside a travel agent's shop, two cyclists – a man and a woman – were about to set off. They had journeyed across Patagonia from Rio and were heading back the same way. A machete, wrapped up in a polythene bag was strapped to the man's crossbar. 'I haven't used it yet,' he said, 'but if anyone came near me in the dead of night I'd whop off their head.' As he and his lady friend pedalled off along the shores of Lake Llanquihue a short, swarthy fellow beckoned to me through the window to enter the shop.

'Is there anything I can do to help you my friend? You are alone?'

I told him I needed a room for the night.

He paused for a moment and looking at the bike said he knew just the place. 'And if you wait a few moments while my girlfriend arrives, I will walk you there.'

Walking past two blocks of houses whose discreetly enclosed salubriousness would have graced any suburb in the world, we arrived at the front door of the one where I was to spend the night. The house was wooden, cream with ivy-green window frames and standard roses growing around a spiked wooden fence surrounding a neatly kept garden. Gabriel had to go and spend a little time with his girlfriend.

'It was she who had chosen me,' he told me, quite unexpectedly, 'to reduce the incidence of disease. This tightly knit community are mostly German. They're riddled with the genetic disharmony of inbreeding,' he said, walking away. 'Thank God for the Chilean.'

A large matronly woman opened the door. She had eyes

like plug sockets and a mouth that could have plunged a drain. Without saying anything, she led me to my room, watching me suspiciously from the corner of her eye. She instructed me to pay immediately and when I gave her two crisp notes, she folded them brusquely, slipped them into her bosom, and left.

From the cold of the outside, the house was warm and I began to sweat after my first day on the road. The room was clean and tidy, brown with varnished timber and smelling of pine. Looking through the window I could see a church, wooden with white sides and a red roof. As I turned to sit on one of the two beds, someone appeared at the door.

'*Señor,*' I said, 'how are you?'

He stared for a moment, quite still, and then as if shaken. 'Yes, I am well.' After that he smiled, a metal brace clasping each tooth as if to hold his jaws together.

'I'll change and then come downstairs,' I said.

He said nothing, preferring instead to stare.

'Change and talk,' I said again, beginning to fumble around for my dictionary. What was that word for 'talk'? I flicked through the pages. '*Hablo,*' I said. 'I would like to talk later.'

He winced, as if it hurt to listen to my ruptured Spanish.

'*Sí,* I understand.' He paused. 'I am dentist, I am Andreas.' He raised his arm and we shook hands. There was another pause, but this time it was as obvious as a pulse in the ear. It was as if our inability to speak easily was too much for him, so he left as invisibly as he arrived.

I began to change, my cycling jersey still looking bright in the light of a long day. So far south, Antarctic shadows were as long as the day was bright. It was beginning to become dark around 11.30pm. Even then, the darkness was not total, for the impatient dawn soon dispelled it.

The living room was rectangular, and large for the size of the house. A table, standing in the middle of the room, was covered in a blue-checked plastic cloth which led to the rested arms of two men in black macs. They stood to leave.

'Off to work,' said the dentist, showing off his teeth, like prison bars, with a sneer. The two men said nothing, attempting only to smile. Fastening their macs they each picked up a slim briefcase and, for a moment more than was comfortable, gazed at me.

'They recruit others at whatever cost to reason,' the dentist said nervously, speaking to me in English. The two men continued to stare. 'They have very much discipline, these

Mormon people, do you understand me?' I nodded, but it was as if he thought that by trying to divert my attention from them he would be more able to appeal to a common instinct that he assumed might exist in me, a foreigner. As I looked towards the dentist, the Mormons moved towards the door.

After they had left the room he appeared more at ease. 'No coffee, no tea, no smoke, no drink, no nothing, no woman,' he said raising his voice, and then with a laugh that erupted from the base of his belly, 'and no noises in the night.' As the front door closed he turned to me and, curling his lips triumphantly, he cursed under his breath. 'But I hear them.'

Andreas must have noticed me glance to the sideboard, against which rested a guitar. He said he would like me to hear a song, it was called 'Dust in the Wind' and he gently began to play.

Through the window the leaves on a weeping willow were still and the moon that stood proudly on the sill was no longer there. The nervous excitement that had compelled me to begin my odyssey in the Americas would also become my tempter. Hard as I might try, I knew I would be seduced away from my pencil-line route that stretched the length of the Andes. The music drifted out of the room and back in again, so sweet did Andreas sing. Often I have sat by my bike wondering whether to talk as a stranger passes or let my thoughts idle in the sun. But after the hellos and the weather and the predictable banter, often the participants are left to plug up the awkwardness of the meeting the best way they can, settling instead for a quick and decent parting.

Andreas was calmer now, like his song, and my thoughts wavered from the essential here and now. I thought of the distance between those standing thinking and someone like myself cycling past. Always there is the weight of an overload of information. It is easy to flounder. Someone once wrote a thesis on the existential quality of the first three seconds of conversation on the telephone; after that I always saw the phone as an instrument of flunked understanding. And sitting by the bike I sometimes evaluated not what I said but how I said it. Talk too little and you are a nervous little person, prey to people who prod with sticks; talk too much and you are neurotic and brash. Gesture beyond the pail and you are to be avoided at all costs. And yet, to stand passively you are nothing. I wondered if to be yourself was an ideal that required an ability to maintain just enough consistency of character not to be thought a fraud.

Andreas's hand froze and then slammed hard on the strings. The sound of a key was heard turning in a lock and Gabriel walked into the room.

'No, continue,' Gabriel implored, but as Andreas placed his guitar by the sideboard, it became obvious that some barrier existed between the two men.

'Ah, you know, I was thinking about what you were saying earlier,' Gabriel looked anxious, 'you know, about Hesse. You know I feel things before they happen. I knew you would come here, because I am here. The Greeks say that when a man is full of himself, everything around him is preserved. Everything around us has a value which is determined by ourselves.'

Andreas was quiet, sidelined in the wake of Gabriel's command of English.

'Take your visit here to Puerto Varas. Before you arrived I imagine this place was, to you, no more than a dot on a map, maybe not even that. And yet you are here, and it exists.' I sensed a collusion of opinion and I wasn't sure if I had one.

'But for me it will soon be a memory which only takes on any meaning when it becomes a few words on a page,' I said. 'Even then, such memories will end their life as an imperfect and biased recollection, passed on, to an unknown reader. Dots on maps conjure up so much more.'

'What is in a dot?' he said forcefully. 'This place is a beauty spot of 23,000 inhabitants on the shore of Lake Llanquihue. The whole countryside is primeval forest, volcanoes with tops of snow surrounding rivers with more blue than you have ever seen. And you tell me of dots. My friend, it depends on the ability of the observer to record well what he will see.'

'I think you have to be more precise. Isn't the ability of the recorder to be in a place and a time which is felt worth recording?'

'So what is worth recording?'

'I suppose what is special.'

'And what is special?'

4

'For me, it is to be here.'

'There is nothing special where you live?'

'Yes, but there I am one of many, here everything is new and fresh, the people are different.'

'You want special people?'

'Isn't everybody a little special?' interrupted Andreas, beginning to grin widely. 'I'm special because I'm a dentist and my teeth are made of tin.'

'Oh yes, that's very special,' Gabriel said sarcastically. 'And what about our landlady? She is as fat as a cow and whenever she leans forwards, farts. She is very special.' Andreas laughed loudly.

'A friend once told me a story of a man who suffered severe nose bleeds for no apparent reason and he only became special after three months,' I said. 'He was washing his face one day when he noticed in the mirror a tentacle flick out of one of his nostrils and when he tried to grab it he missed. When he eventually caught a grip, he nearly pulled out half his brains trying to persuade a buffalo leech to evacuate his nose.'

'Pretty special leech ah?' said Andreas, happy to mock his rival.

'Special nose,' I said.

'Impossible,' Gabriel shouted curtly. 'Don't talk to me of such nonsense. And as you have so little time I want to tell you that I am a very special person. There is no one else like me in the world. I think differently to these people.' Gabriel was strangely at ease, the words as rehearsed as the smoke that hung like a smog around his finely trimmed beard. He smoked with such assurance. 'I will tell you all you need to know about this area,' and he pointed to the church I'd noticed from my bedroom. 'That church was built . . .' he started to say, but I stopped listening. It was now more restful to be quiet, the sun had long ago slipped into dusk and the chill of night . . . 'It was built with Cypress trees that took over 3,500 years to grow . . . 30 per cent of the people here in the Tenth Region are German . . . 70 per cent of all Chile's milk comes from here . . . It's the most expensive town in Chile and in this tiny and insignificant little place there are more Mercedes cars per capita than anywhere else from here to Arica . . .' He paused. 'Is that not special?'

Gabriel eventually became quiet so I excused myself on the pretext that something on my bicycle needed adjusting. It was partly the truth, but more than that, this stocky man had spent

5

the evening projecting a smug self-belief that had begun to undermine my own.

Fiddling with my sprockets was not really my idea of fun, but pulling off errant strands of handlebar tape that had begun to make the bike look tatty was a worthwhile exercise. Weeks had passed by on journeys like this when I hadn't even wiped the chain clean. A tired and innocent hope that all things work out for the best has accompanied me in the jungles and the deserts; I had no reason to disbelieve in mountains.

The hallway where I kept the bike was gloomy. A single stained-glass window entertained what little light could be gleaned from a full moon, flinging it among the dust by the stairs. The bike looked neglected where it stood so I wheeled it away from moonshadows that began to creep up the wall. In an instant the spokes radiated light to precision-cut wheel rims that had hardly been marked by brake rubbers, so new was the journey. Black tyres gripped wheels that, forging along the length of the majestic Andes, would rotate millions of times. Each pedal stroke would thrust the tread into the ground, and the impact of every upturned stone I would feel in my bones. The nuts were tight and the body of the frame solid but sleek. This was a very sleek bike. I had painted it blue for the sky, yellow for the sun and red for the raging desert – not for battle but to complement all the colours that a country might throw at me. I'd spent months thinking about this journey, trying to attune myself to the spirit of the Andes. There was no idealistic desire to tread any path to self-discovery, just a realistic swopping of one form of solitude for another. The physical preparation was haphazard and a further long weekend was spent packing essential equipment into my pannier bags. As I would spend most nights sleeping on the side of the road, a sleeping bag was, until the end of the South American summer, my new home. Other useful objects, like cameras, clothes and toothpaste, jockeyed for position as best they could; but my documentation was stored in the zip pocket of my front left pannier, and for reasons of safety, whether I was standing, sitting, sleeping or shitting, would never be more than arm's length from me. As the dust travelled along rays of moonlight squeezed needle-like and sharp, I had at last begun to acquaint myself with my machine.

Gabriel insisted we go to the casino. It was, he said, all the rage. All the smart people of Puerto Varas would be there. He looked around at the landlady who had entered the room from the kitchen and continued rather gracelessly, 'But those who stink of their own toilet are not allowed in.' The landlady glared at Gabriel and, as I got up to leave, a plate thumped on to the table. She had prepared me a little supper: weary stew and a cup of dying tea. When I politely declined she shrugged her shoulders and gave it to the dog.

'The landlady,' Andreas whispered to me, 'regards Gabriel as the sort of life that slops around the gutter. He thinks she is mad and a whore.'

Gabriel switched on the ignition and the car screeched as the tyres started to burn. Andreas screamed excitedly and we began to flash past shop windows, milliseconds at a time, until we reached the exact point of darkness where I knew we were out of town.

The casino was a bore. Girls in skin-tight pink trousers lack-eyed around fat-jowled German women with mushy red lips. The men looked like war criminals; nicely tanned, always smiling with their gold teeth. Arcaded hallways led to columned rooms where the not-so-rich played bingo. But it was the roulette wheel that had the business stacked around its sides. Chips that represented a year's work for a peasant, lost or won on the chance of a dice. But is that not the game of the immigrant? That at each change of political climate they risk being allowed to keep what they say they have strived for, or are stripped naked and thrown on to the land. These people in their trilbys were living for now, sauntering collectively and charmlessly. Hispanics who try to emigrate to the United States are called 'wetbacks' on account of many of them sweating their way illegally across the Mexican border. In this closed German community, Gabriel is a wetback in his own country, and until he is able to sit comfortably under a trilby, will always have the sweat on his back.

TWO

The following morning I said goodbye to Gabriel and Andreas. They tried to persuade me to stay. It was the Saturday dance at the casino, they said. All the more reason to go, and what did I think of the girls in the pink trousers? I said I wanted to be on my bike, to ride slowly to Puerto Montt.

I was cycling, 665 miles from Santiago, on the Pan American Highway that stretched from Alaska, from Prudhoe Bay next to Deadhorse overlooking the Beaufort Sea, stretching halfway around the world to the town of Castro on an island called Chiloe. Only 156 miles long and 31 miles wide, Chiloe was just a short ferry ride away from Puerto Montt, the capital of the Tenth Region. The highway is 12,000 miles long and, apart from a gap of two or three hundred miles south of Panama in Central America, it is continuous. I had planned to ride from the southernmost tip of the Americas to the Equator, from Ushuaia on Tierra del Fuego to Quito in Ecuador. I had dreamed of the isolation that sat just above Cape Horn, of Darwin and Fitzroy, the Bridges family who settled on the island with the Yaghan and Ona Indians; I imagined the expanse of Patagonia, the 153 Welsh settlers that anchored the clipper *Mimosa* in New Bay, off the coast of Argentina. They were poor but they were armed with the hope that a better life awaited them there. I pictured blue skies that pressed against the cutting edge of the crest of the Andes, dotted, I'd hoped, with the silhouettes of condors. In the midst of a whistling wind that blew sweet smells of warming heather, I cycled out on a South American summer morning.

The wind was warm and blowing from the north. Soon, when times and schedules were no longer important, the days would scramble out of position and in my mind not have any particular order. But on the second day of the journey that was not yet likely to happen. Every mile or so I stopped and sat astride the bike, marvelling at everything I saw. Plovers bleated somewhere in acres of thorny scrub that grew around pockets of *meseta* bushes. In between the rest stops I raced shadows the size of houses, sent down by rolling clouds that scurried across the sky. Clouds would probably be my only constant companion as I crossed the barrenness of Patagonia.

Here and there in Puerto Montt, I rode past houses faced with unpainted shingles, slats covering the exterior walls, and, in the Alpine manner, high-pitched roofs and quaint balconies. Looking for a suitable overnight stopover, I began to sense that there was a cheaper part of the town. The Andean journey in parts is a major travellers' highway but rest houses are still sparse. A local suggested 'Uncle Renato's' on the road Guillermo 621 and after 600 yards up an unmade track I found a small stout gentleman sitting outside his house.

'Floor for rent,' he shouted, 'we do the best rates in town.' He stood up to welcome me, short stocky arms grabbed me warmly. 'I am Uncle Renato and you have been looking for me, yes?' He had a large head, sat square on his shoulders, with nothing to separate the two. He put his arm around me, making it awkward to walk, but by pretending to be in a three-legged race, we made it slowly up the garden path. 'You are Christian?' Uncle Renato looked at me searchingly.

'I wouldn't hurt a fly,' I said (lying – I hate flies).

'But that doesn't make you Christian.' I nodded in agreement.

The house was divided into two rooms downstairs, an eating room and another room with a beautifully polished floor on which to sleep. 'We are Pentecostals in this house,' and he gestured with his arm towards what he wanted me to see. The pictures on the wall suggested the piety of a Christian household in the modern-day world – Jesus walking through the Garden of Gesetheme in 3-D. Pulling me into the kitchen he said 'Eat, eat,' and a plate of potato soup was placed on the table in front of me. A black-haired girl sat on the other side.

'Another convert?' she said.

I shook my head. When she enquired about my purpose here I told her that I was from Europe, trying to shield her and myself from a tedious repetition of my journey. I asked her what she did.

'I am poet,' she said, fingering back hair which was as unkempt as I imagined poets' hair to be. 'I have been writing in Europe, in France. What a delight.' A potato dropped off my spoon and splattered into the bowl of gravy. 'When I was twenty years,' she continued, 'I came back from my studio. There I had been a rationalist.'

'What's that?' I asked.

'Oh it's a long story, but let us say that my father was a little spiritual and my mother was not, so I became a little confused. They sent me away to a special hospital where my mind lost its hold. But I am better now.' She paused. 'Do you want to hear one of my poems? I have it this minute finished . . . but I think it will lose something in the translation.'

I nodded.

'Well, here it is:

> "For Chile first
> My bloomy roof is you
> With your blue sky
> With the snow in the cordilliera
> With your star.
>
> For Chile second,
> For to leave in the dream of the night
> The beginning of the day
> I need his sky blue eyes as if they were mine
> His masculine face appearing in my face
> And his hands holding my hands." '

It was market day and fishermen heaved nets that shivered with eel and the South Pacific. At the far end of town the marketeers at Angelmo, Puerto Montt's harbour, sat around wooden boxes that dripped with the stink of fish warming in the sun. Half the town seemed to jam the corridors of fly-blown stalls and all that could be seen was a sea of shopping bags. Poked and picked at among the oily catch, octopus the size of a hand and shellfish by the ton were pressed to a hundred faces and then slopped back on to the floor or wrapped in crinkly brown paper.

The breeze whistled around the quay, pushing an army of clouds through the path of the sun. My poet friend suggested

1   The ship Evangelista *carrying trucks and a few passengers to Puerto Natales, the only Chilean route to Tierra del Fuego.*

2   *Riding into the hold of the* Evangelista *at Puerto Montt, I felt the adventure was at last beginning. The route would hug one of the most inhospitable coastlines in the world.*

3 *The view from Puerto Natales was of a small slice of the Andes, one of the most beautiful views in the world.*

4 *Tommy Dick at his home by the road to Punta Arenas. He had a habit of smiling, or perhaps wasn't accustomed to having his photograph taken.*

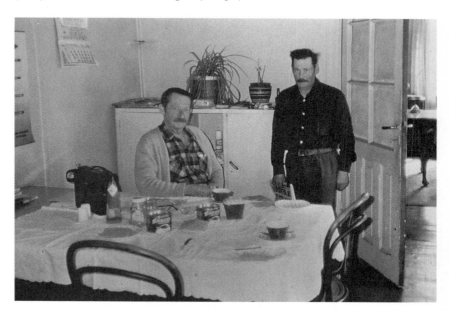

5   Torres del Paine National Park.

6   *Uncle Beetle and canary at Estancia Viamonte. The canary was Beetle's pride and joy. He talked about this bird above all things but was rather worried that the bird's ill health would soon prove terminal.*

7 and 8   *Ushuaia. From a distance, flanked by mountains, it looks as it is, a small town far from anywhere. It is also the most southerly town in the world.*

8

she guide me around town and, after introducing herself as Patricia Huaira Pamushka – the Mapuche Indian name for 'daughter of the wind' – we walked in and out of shadows, me wheeling my bike. The wind first blew her hair, loose strands whiplashing around large eyes and ruby lips, and then blew her. Buffeted between the street and the sea she somehow fitted with the wind, her body quivering and embracing, interlocking with something that I couldn't see. She said that 'the invisible waves' were violent with her. 'They force open a space in my thoughts, to gather and become quiet,' she said. 'The wind for me is a force that cuts through glaciers and warms in the Atacama. It is up and down, big and small, sometimes here and sometimes not.' She spoke as poets do, wth a self-possessed blarney, so in such a context it made sense. Yet elsewhere there was a feeling of larceny in the wind as it wrenched around the concrete of the city, pummelling people's faces into submission. 'Ah, the wind,' was all I heard her say, and with long deep draughts she gulped in the air.

We walked along the harbour, drank tea and watched the circle of *bandurrias* (lute) players around the Old Tree which was sited in the courtyard of a school in the centre of town. With its thick gnarled trunk and curling branches that had reached out for a thousand years, this was no ordinary tree.

'This tree has a great mystery,' she breathed quietly. 'It is a tree that has no flowers and yet once a year it gives fruit.' As if waiting, and sheltered as it was, so secretly from the wind, not a leaf moved. 'Only on the 23rd of June, no other time, does it become bloomy. Ah, but so strange and beautiful,' and Patricia looked bewitched. 'If you have the force to be there at night, the devil gives you knowledge of things that you would not normally know.'

Later that afternoon I rode alone along the promenade to Angelmo, the harbour of Puerto Montt. Stalls selling trinkets on the sea side of the road lined the two-mile route to the edge of town, which in turn led to the entrance of a large fish shed. And stuck like clams around the hull of one of the boats in the harbour, the walls of the shed were cluttered with miniature restaurants smelling of the sea. By chance I sat inside one with a larger room, the walls covered with posters of sporting heroes. A sign outside advertised 'The Café of Signor Hernandez'.

A man the size of an ox leant carefully over me, pointing to the stove on which a pan bubbled and popped. He smiled and then spoke, but not in the way that humans can understand. The words of Signor Hernandez came from lower down in the body. Sharp groans that growled and twisted, as if stored in his stomach, were shrill and plaintive when they reached the outside world. He had never been able to talk, but from the speed of his flickering eyes it was obvious he was as sharp as a fox. For listening he used elephant's ears, the lobes pulled down by the fingers of deformity and stretched down his cheeks. Across his forehead, eyebrows joined as on the face of a wolf. His teeth were broken, pointed and sharp.

He nodded yes to me, yes, did I want the soup? I nodded back and beckoned for a drink. He pointed to the kettle. And bread? I broke the air with my hands, I waited a moment and, yes, he had seen me and smiled. I motioned to stir a spoon in my cup and in a blink he brought me sugar; I spread an imaginary knife on my bread, and he responded with foil-wrapped packs of butter. He skitted and jumped from kettle to table, barking his orders, licking his lips, shouting, laughing with a thumping cry, but then he stood and, with cocked head, watched me eat; the sugar and butter and tea were all in place and everything was in order. For a moment he was quiet as a mouse, still as the wolf, dry and thirsty, as if smelling water in a parched wind. Grinding his clenched teeth, his face crumpled in momentary frustration before he began to serve me pudding. I knew that he wanted to talk, and he knew that he couldn't. Yet he had taught me that in a faraway place where there is more to talking than talking, it is perhaps better to be like the fox or the mouse.

I had been waiting in Puerto Montt for several days, waiting for the departure of the ferry *Evangelista*. Deep in the Province of Magallanes in the 12th Region my cycling would begin. It would take four days to sail along the coast of the Chilean Antarctic Archipelago, where acts of daring had become associated to the rocks around which we would pass.

The ferry was due to depart the next day so I sat on a bench that overlooked the harbour. Curving around a nest of eucalyptus trees out to sea, a small island sat seductively.

'Yes, it ees an island.' I turned to see Patricia standing beside me. 'It ees not so easy to see that the water goes all around its shores. Yes, we take a boat and have a closer look.'

We walked to the harbour wall where she spoke to one of the fishermen.

'You will look after his bicycle?' she said to one of the fishermen who nodded. Another beckoned us down by way of steps scratched into a section of the wall that sloped down to the sea. He would become our ferryman. Setting the oars in the rowlocks he pointed the bow away from shore and, straightening his back, began to pull. We heaved in a light swell and so close were we to the *Evangelista* that I could smell the waves that bounced off her bow.

It was a short distance away from the shore and after climbing out of the boat we walked up to the top of the island. I could hear the laughter of men through glassless windows, that almost seemed to have grown in the timbers of a white-fronted hotel. Surrounded by a coven of eucalyptus trees, their shiny green leaves became dull as they reflected storm clouds that were beginning to gather. We talked quietly, drinking red wine from the heartland.

However, Patricia became silent now and I felt I'd disarmed her by introducing a little of the ordinary into the late afternoon. Feeling redundant I went into the bar to buy another bottle when one of four men sitting by the window called me over to drink with them.

I looked around and saw an honest face, round and shiny. His hair was short and he was sufficiently immaculate, in his worsted tweed jumper, to be in the navy. Forgetting about my companion for a few moments I sat at the table. 'You have travelled far,' he said, smiling.

'How do you know?'

'Anybody who travels to Chile has travelled far,' he laughed and offered me a little wine, 'and where is your friend?'

'Oh, Patricia,' I reddened.

'Bring in your friend,' he said.

I got up and from the door called to her. Resignedly, she eased herself upright to stand unsteadily into the wind, then made her way towards the bar.

The clean-cut man was called Roberto, and he smiled when Patricia sat at the table. 'In Chile they say if the wine is good, let it be drunk.' As gusts of wind began to snap at the branches of trees that stood between us and the harbour, the loss of light had sapped away the colour, turning everything into a shade of blue and grey. Clouds full of the sea hung darkly on the rim of hills that guarded the town. The lights of the *Evange-*

lista shifted in the air as everything began to scurry in the wake of the impending storm. The evening talk slowly gathered momentum.

'I was in Newcastle for seven months and there it was good, everything was accessible. And the woman, they are so beautiful.' Roberto paused for a moment and shivered, it was chilly so far south. 'But they say the English men are so cold. That they do not care about their sensitivity. How they feel in the bed?'

'Play the guitar, Roberto,' one of the other men shouted. 'Sing now and talk later.' I hadn't noticed the guitar standing next to the adjoining table.

'And you know,' Roberto continued, picking up the guitar in a single, sweeping motion, 'we attend to their needs, open doors, pay for their drinks. Ah yes, but you know, I was in love with an English girl and for three years we corresponded. It is wonderful and a sad thing this love. I was very sad to leave.' As if summoning a little romantic courage he began to play a song called 'Si Vas Para Chile'. He said the song would speak of strangers from faraway lands that are made welcome in Chile, one of the most beautiful countries in the world.

'Tell me before I begin, have you loved?' He strummed quietly until I gave him my answer. Here was a man who spoke from his heart, and compared with him I felt cold and rhymeless.

'Yes,' I said, 'and I agree with you about the sadness.'

THREE

The ferry *Evangelista* was similar to any of those that drone monotonously across the English Channel. The bow was hydraulically to allow diesel-spattered trucks into the belly of the ship. When everything was loaded, the few passengers who had been lucky enough to secure a ticket shuffled through whatever space was left. I wouldn't need my bike until we docked so I locked it to a metal pipe and removed the panniers.

The point of disembarkation would be Puerto Natales, beyond which the archipelago of Antarctic islands would continue towards one of the most inhospitable inhabited areas on earth – Tierra del Fuego – and then Cape Horn. Depending on the weather, the four-day journey could last a week. So far south, the sun manages to penetrate the thick rolling storm clouds for less than two months of the year. This land, savage by reputation and desolate by geographical design, would present the first real physical challenge of the journey. I was not a sailor and simply imagined that we would slowly edge ourselves out of sight of land only to be squeezed through endless cliff-faced channels beset by squalls and a raging, ship-eating sea. We were to ease our way between the island of Chiloe and the mainland, then down the Moraleda, Mesier, Inocentes and Smyth channels and with luck and a following wind berth safely at the end of the voyage.

At right angles to the port hole and opposite a small washbasin and wardrobe there were two bunk-beds. I chose the bottom bed, thinking that if the swell were to fling me to the ground I'd probably survive the fall. To be always vigilant has never been a family motto, but in cyclist-speak, woe are they who bloody a nose by riding down a gridhole. Nobody in my family had ever embarked on a journey by ship and my sense of the sea prevailed on me to leave my life in the hands of the captain. He, standing with his electronic navigational aids, may not have been a Fitzroy scrutinising his charts 'with all its stars to mark the rocks, looking like a map of part of the heavens rather than part of the earth', but the implicit trust that Fitzroy's authority inspired in Darwin was not unlike my own. Resting my saddlebags on the bed, I settled myself in a space around them and fell asleep. Only briefly, when the rumble of the engines purred into my doze, did I awake. Through the porthole I saw the men of the other ship in the harbour, the *Tierra del Fuego*, shout and salute. A deep earthy horn blasted its response and as Tenglo Island and the shore-line of the town began its journey to the horizon I fell back on to my bed and slept until morning.

That night and all the following day I did not stir from my bed. A strange exhaustion had overtaken me, as if I needed to sleep in readiness for a time when, without a bed, I would wish that were possible. Beneath me I felt the roll of the ocean sifting in and out of a deep sombre dream that had the nightmarish quality of a monster.

I sat alone on the top deck, unmoving, catatonic almost, sleepy with the cold which began to sting and pierce. On the edge of a dizzy sea, panting waves hit the bow, funnelling us through the corridor of islands that grew closer, so I could see where the shore met the rabid tide. Towering peaks, when not obscured by cloud, had icy-blue tops and waterfalls that cascaded from a height of perhaps 1,500ft. The distance and the waves obscured their sound. They were silent in a secret land. High up they hid in the forests, only to burst through a gap in the woodwork halfway down, dashing into the channel below, the vestigial meltwater from the Patagonian icecap. Above the surf and below trees that poked like matchsticks from the shadows of crevice walls, a rim of salt divided the two. Against all this, wavelets unfurled to flick into platelets of surf.

Wallowing heavily, the *Evangelista* heaved as storm clouds gathered. I looked out over the bow and recognised the genesis of a drunken sea that, except for a tint of blue, was devoid of colour. As we edged forward, a little boat on the cruel flange of a tempest, I wondered how it must have been to chart these waters, how some of the greatest chapters in history have been written as a consequence of seemingly insignificant incidents. The charting of this coastline by Captain Fitzroy and Charles

Darwin spawned a branch of scientific enquiry that was to revolutionise the way man thought about his existence.

After four days at sea, the *Evangelista* docked at Puerto Natales. Dark clouds heaped on the far side of Last Hope Sound threatened at once the sun drying the tops of scabby tin roofs. As I wheeled my bike on to the quay, a boy of about nineteen grabbed my arm. ' *Sí*, bed, I have,' and with wide eyes and clumsy movements he edged me nearer to his house, chatting constantly.

Casting a glance I could seek stark, glaciated peaks reflected in a calm tongue of sea. It wasn't necessary to look, the chill wind had already bitten into my lungs. The boy pulled me further from the boat. His abrupt hospitality camouflaged his fear and made people stare. Having crossed such huge lands, a stranger is received with pity and awe by the inhabitants. Pity for being so far from home; awe for coming so far to be here. Trailing this boy I wandered through streets lined with wooden houses, and I could breathe in the pine. Pushing the bike it felt balanced and good, the handlebars turning well under the weight of the front panniers. I desired more than anything to stretch my legs astride my horse, but I was more patient now, accepting what might happen instead of forming events.

Gently eased through a wooden porch and then a corridor, I was led to a kitchen warmed by a wood-burning stove, smoke trickling between its circular brim. Yellow paint had peeled like spiragira, curled and dead in clumps on the floor. The boy poured the contents of the kettle into a mug and mixed the last of what appeared to be grass. 'Only tepid water, never too hot,' the boy said. '*Mate*, it keeps you going all day but never stops you sleeping at night.' Inserting a metal straw into the drink he became quiet, and, like a baby suckling, fell into a torpor.

In the quietness I thought of the journey that lay ahead: riding into the wind, crouching into busy rain, the cold night sky and another fragment of universe with which I wasn't yet acquainted. It was time to prepare. To realise that the journey was going to be long and hard and that if I wasn't ready for the job, the job would not be finished. The warmth of the stove reminded me of the cold outside. It was summer and the night was grim-faced.

The boy looked up, unblinking and a little legless. 'I am nervous when I don't drink my *mate*. I am *mate* drinker.' As if waking, the next twenty minutes he danced and sang, banged a drum with the gusto of a rock-star, fiddled with my bike, made more tea and then slumped down in a heap.

'Ah, so you've met my son have you?' A small roundish lady came into the room and after taking off her headscarf, rubbed my hands in hers. 'You are nice and warm, and he is *such* an enthusiastic boy.' She paused to take off her coat. 'He's epileptic you know and this is how he is. Excitable.' Taking off her shoes she replaced them with slippers, and putting the kettle on the stove she asked me to sit down by the fire where we could have a cup of tea and perhaps a little chat.

'I used to be a nun you know,' she said quite simply, 'and I can tell you, he came as quite a shock.'

That evening I pored over my maps, checking the route to Punta Arenas, wondering from which corner of this hard land the wind would blow. It was 150 miles to this, the last large settlement before I would cross the Strait of Magellan. To compose the journey properly, I would wait a day, have a look around, and like a starling take on a disguise and be ready for whatever the next day might bring. Looking out of the window I could see a three-quarter full moon rise over pencil-sharp mountains.

Shutters covering the windows of the house were already beginning to bang, as the fire glowed. I sat with my elbows supported by an adjoining table, enough to tease the rest of the room with a hunchback's shadow. The mantle lamp hissed but the light was still. I must have been with my maps for hours. Suddenly, the back door was flung open by a tank-headed man, as tall as he was broad, and laughing. Under his arm a sheep rolled its eyes.

'Visitors eh?' and his laughter sneered. Throwing the animal into the corner of the room, its legs trussed to keep it immobile, he rolled up the shirt sleeve of one arm. 'Muscle, muscle, yes,' he said and with a face that could easily misunderstand, flexed his arm with a rigour that was threatening. He pulled out a knife and brandished it in front of my face. It remained so for an instant too long. Moving quickly to the corner he picked up the sheep and pressed the blade deep into its neck. The

18

sheep pissed. 'Now you take a colour photo,' he says, 'now, or maybe tomorrow.'

Smiling like a Rottweiler, his teeth were spaced to kill. A well-defined gap between each tooth was the occasional resting ground for a fat tongue that got in the way of what he wanted to say. His laughter edged towards mania. I excused myself and made to retire to my room. 'Tomorrow,' he taunted and leaving the kitchen I closed the door behind me.

My bike stood by the window; a piece of string fastened it to a chair. I moved the bike and the chair in front of my door which opened inwards. Should the door open, the bike would topple and the chair would clatter to the floor. On a journey I liked most people but trusted few. I was the supreme paranoid and excellent in my art. Survival on the road is as much a matter of camouflage as a perfect ability to flee. The darkness of the room, interrupted only by the light from the kitchen and the sound of subdued laughter creeping under the door, was perfect for such thoughts. So hidden, I could no longer keep awake, yet as an uneasy doze drifted into a light sleep I thought I heard the door widen. There were footsteps to my bed.

As my hair began to bristle I knew I was being touched. My burglar alarm had never yet failed, until that night. Feeling my hair being brushed, soothingly, my eyes opened as I shot upright, sweating, into the startled arms of the *mate* drinker. He was smiling like an off-duty angel and although his eyes were open I didn't think he was seeing. He groaned like a bitch on heat. Pulling back my covers he slid one of his legs beside me, when I grasped his arm. 'Me *mate*-drinker, me remember you.' Half sitting on the bed he raised his other leg as I pulled him vigorously towards me, to whisper in his ear.

'I have something to say to you in English because I don't know the Spanish,' and closing two fingers like scissors, 'so if you try and get any closer, I'll cut off your dick.'

'Oh, there he is,' his mother hushed, stepping over my bike to pull him away, 'he wants only to make friends, make sure everyone is in their rooms and is OK, it is his way.' The boy was led into the corridor and my door closed. The light in the kitchen was switched off. Domestic noises over, the house was now silent. I *did* put the bike against the door and the chair did *not* crash. So this ghostly little man either walked through the door or wriggled his way through the gap beneath. There was no other way into the room.

19

Eduardo Scott was the son of British emigrées. Moustachioed and wearing a baseball hat, he lived just down the road. His mother was born on the Falklands in 1890 and his father in Somerset around the same time. 'Dad died before I was born. He worked in the cookhouse with my grandfather and, after journeying to Punta Arenas, mother had to orphan my two brothers. She was pregnant with me and had to work as a chambermaid.' Eduardo was one of the last living examples of settlers that I could find. He talked about Cecilia Everhard who in 1894 started the first sheep farm in Puerto Natales, from which an industry grew to supply wool across the Atlantic. He talked about horse-breaking, wild horses, bronco-riding.

When he was thirteen years old he pinched the back of the beast with his spindly legs as hard as dear life itself. He boxed with the champion of the British Navy and learnt two years after the fight that he'd broken the poor chap's nose. He said he once beat the living daylights out of the man who eventually became the·second champion of the whole of Chile. 'I've got an aunt in Andover, Florence Pissy. Look, they sent me a postcard.' It was the Ship Inn in Porlock. He told me to go and see an old friend of his on the road to Punta Arenas. 'Go and see Tommy Dick at Penitentes, he'll look after you.'

The following day I began my journey to Punta Arenas. Everything was behind me now, on the first day's journey by bike. The handlebars were cold and as I looked down at my front wheel, and then my pedals, hovering on the first pedal turn of the journey . . . and then . . . head up . . . I was on my way.

I began to speed on a machine that my imagination had given a little majesty. I felt like Stokes commandeering the *Beagle* in a fair wind, and, whatever should happen later in the journey, I was for the moment in control at the helm. Climbing away from the town on the edge of a bay the colour of beryl, I felt the sunshine soften the chill of the morning. The road undulated and straightened, at first dodging around scrub embedded into wind-parched plains, later bludgeoning forward with the strength of a railway track. That on each side

9 *Signor Herendez, Puerto Montt. He couldn't speak, but he employed every gesture needed to run a restaurant and make you feel welcome. The conversation I had with him was as articulate as any I have known.*

10 *Fishing boat near Puerto Natales. Clustered patiently for a sale. All Chilean Pacific fish could be bought still wriggling in the net.*

11 *Torres del Paine National Park, a site of great beauty little known outside Chile.*

of the road I could see every shade of green and brown made it difficult sometimes to distinguish between the two. Canaries, yellow as the sun, zipped about the ground in the wake of black-necked swans and young grey geese airing early morning feathers. Lesser rheas, here called Nandus, in their make-believe world, strutted as goblins might from side to side, arching strong necks to flee into a wind strong from the Atlantic.

It was exciting being on the road, hearing my wheels flush forward, the chain purring effortlessly on the cogs. The absence of traffic reminded me that this barren land was not a flattened Dartmoor; the cold assured me I was not in Niger where the sun was hot until dusk or the brown-green flatlands of Burundi that stretch down to Tanzania. I was a day's ride from a strait of water so steeped in the history of men opening up unknown lands, it compared wonderfully with the Bosporus or the Nile.

FOUR

The road to Punta Arenas swept through a plain of cascading heather, a vein of lead through the purple. On the road, faraway from home, I was at ease. Should I be forced away from the road which I understood, the indefinable worth of my journey would further elude me. I couldn't do as Magellan and no longer wanted to. I ate, snoozed, and breathed on the road. I was a part of the road, shuffling along insect-like, becoming the colour of the road, dusty and grey. Cycling alone requires at least a sense of survival by camouflage, a practised control of eyes and face. The uncertain flicker of an eye can mean as much as a blush or show of panic when riding past *nandoos* and *guanaco*, startling them to look up. Lorries likewise did the same to me.

I stopped for lunch at a hotel, midway between Puerto Natales and Punta Arenas. Ordering coffee and a ham sandwich I turned to watch the *nandoos* I knew as *rheas*. The barman pointed out the females foraging for their young.

'The men they just hang around all day on them eggs,' the barman said, edging towards the window.

'And then?' I asked.

'And then they hatch,' the barman said, taking his cue for tourist-tattle. 'The chicks they stay with their fathers because it is the mothers they run so fast.'

'Then?'

'They group or they die, Signor. The *kaikin*, the hawks, Signor, they pull the stragglers to pieces.' Nearby, *guanacos* basked in the warm sun, their smooth fur, brown as autumn fern. Commonplace in the region, they had necks like llamas, heads like deer and bodies like fat goats. Here the inverse chauvinism of the *nandoos* is reversed with the male adopting the unusual trend of disappearing when the siblings arrive. As I watched the foraging through the window, the sound of air brakes broke the quiet air and a coachload of tourists heaved into the bar.

The wind blew me along as if I were a sparrow. The wheels flushed a path through the air and my legs whirred the pedals like the bottom half of a steamer duck. All afternoon I rode hard and strong, making use of every blow of the wind. For long periods the road would be mine, punctuated by the odd lorry thrashing its way to the bottom of the world. As the days passed I began to feel the trucks getting closer before I heard them. Built on a land of marsh and bog the road would vibrate under the strain of so much tyre and load. Descending to a road block 70 miles from Puerto Natales at Moro Chico, I stopped overlooking a shallow river that twinkled next to a policeman's hut. I asked the guard if he knew Tommy Dick. He said he did and I was told to ride two more miles and take the next right before the crest of a hill and there I would see a sign marked Río Penitentes.

From the road there was no view of any *estancia* buildings but, passing through an open gate, I bumped down a gravel track that wound deep into a valley. And there in the distance like some Scottish mansion house it stood magnificently.

Tommy Dick lived with his wife in a rambling series of rooms adjacent to the house. When I told him Eduardo Scott had sent me, he smiled and asked me if I'd like some tea and perhaps teacakes. 'After all, dear boy, it is four o'clock.'

Tommy looked tired. His face, hanging around a drooping moustache, was lined with the look of someone exiled from a homeland he had never seen. A dusty wall clock tapped out gently the long hours while the rest of the kitchen surrounded a table scrubbed like a butcher's bench. Tommy's wife placed before me my tea and I was treated in the manner of an honoured guest. It was obvious I was here to listen to a story.

'My grandparents on my mother's side were from Inverness and the farm was founded in 1896 by Alexander Morrison,' he said, concentrating on a patchwork of dusty memories. 'On my father's side, well, they were from Cotebridge close to Glasgow, and he came here in 1910.' Tommy's wife operated the kitchen briskly and asked me if I wanted more tea.

23

'He came out here to receive a consignment of coal, if I remember rightly, and when it arrived they opened the hatches and by some spontaneous combustion, started a fire.' He paused. 'Ha . . . you see, instead of closing the hatches and beaching the ship they panicked and lost the lot.' Tommy's father died in 1952 and was responsible for much of the family fortunes, such that they were. The upkeep of the main house was too much for Tommy's ailing health so it was now being run as a hotel, but custom was slow.

'He was so clever,' Tommy continued. 'He kept inventories for local farms, hauled lumber to the Argentine coast and bales of wool back to Tierra del Fuego. He had a saw mill, a crab factory, a sheep dip factory, oh, so many things,' he said, tailing off. Tommy's mother, born and educated in Glasgow, travelled back to the UK every two years, but for Tommy that was just a dream.

Looking out of the window, Tommy spotted a duck flapping over the garden. 'Black-necked swans,' he said. 'They're like ducks you know, it's the Coscorova swan that's completely white.'

I asked him about other birds that live here.

'Well, we have the upland geese. The male is white and the female black, except the young which are grey.' Sitting up he looked less languid. 'And then there's the Andean condor which I'm sure you know. You see them as black dots but I tell you they can carry off a lamb. And then we have wild canaries as yellow as the sun and did you see the little London sparrow?' I nodded and said they made me feel homesick. 'Nice little fellers the sparrow,' he said to himself, looking away.

Invited to stay for the night, I was shown my room. The bed let me sink almost to the floor, enveloping me with hand-sewn quilts and pillows that every so often became just that much smaller with the escape of yet another feather.

That evening we talked about the Chilean involvement in the Falklands War. Sitting around the fire I looked out of the window and wished it were dark. It would be winter back in England and summer here, and perversely I felt deprived of my long, miserable nights. Long days were too demanding for me: there was so much time to negotiate, so many things you felt you had to do.

24

'You know of the saga of the ditched helicopter?' he asked.

I was startled. 'I didn't follow the war,' I said. 'I knew it had something to do with principle but it seemed so futile.'

'The implications were terrible, young man, you should know. But the helicopter was half-submerged in the Strait and where were the crew? They were found walking along the road, clean-shaven for a week. Some say they had been hidden in my barn.' His eyes twinkled but I was suspicious of such information proferred so easily. There was a silence.

'Had they?' I asked. He looked hard at me, then down at a cigarette he had just lit, and said nothing.

'Oh stop it, darling,' Mrs Dick said to her husband, stepping into the living room from the kitchen. 'He doesn't want to hear all this, do you.' And turning to me, 'Anyway we've got a nice fresh salmon, tossed salad and a lovely chocolate dessert for afters, yes.' So ushering us into our places around a table dressed for dinner, we sat down to eat. But Tommy's face was set.

'If Argentina had come here first they would have walked in easily, but I tell you, there would have been an uprising. Every Argentine with a Chilean heart, third even fourth generation emigrées would have revolted.' No longer looking at me, and as if examining his own fight within, he began quietly. 'From here to Bia Blanco, the gas and oil would have moved in from Puerto Montt.' His voice rose in crescendo. 'The Argentinians are basically Italian in nature and they do not have a warlike mentality. I tell you,' he said loudly, thumping the table, 'they only make a lot of noise,' and falling back into his seat he looked a little red in the face.

All the following day I cycled, the sun breaking through a crisp cross wind. In front of me, the road dissected the horizon into two evenly uninteresting halves, across which I knew I had to go.

As the sun began to set, the outskirts of Punta Arenas presented themselves like a freshly ironed skirt. The road was laced with poplars and larch through which could be seen neatly fenced-off areas around *frigerificos* and container bays with wool sheds storing fleece. Until the discovery of oil – Tierra del Fuego and north of the Magellan Strait produce all Chilean oil – the breeding of sheep was the most important industry. A large British colony at one time lived here, but it was now diminishing to nothing. At almost equal distance from the Atlantic and Pacific Oceans, 1,394 nautical miles from Buenos Aires and 1,432 from Valparaiso, Punta Arenas is the most southerly city in Chile, busy yet unassuming, and has a position of almost unrivalled military significance, standing sentinel over the islands of the South Atlantic.

My only contact was Enrique, a small man with a head as polished as a skinned rabbit, who was in charge of tourism.

'If you like,' he said, sitting at his desk extolling the virtues of Chile, 'I will ask my driver to take you to the Torres del Paine, the most magnificent national park in the world.' I accepted his invitation and was expected to be ready to leave the following day. 'In the mean time,' he said, 'as a result of you appearing in our paper yesterday, a local socialite, Mrs King, has offered you her hospitality tonight should you so wish.'

Anybody who is simply anybody is invited around for tea at Joyce E. King's place on the outskirts of P.A.. Large and businesslike with a flock of white hair, she was to the rest of her genus what a combine harvester is to a scythe. While her husband worked as president of an oil company she worked with the poor and needy, supplying books, as she said, 'to the illiterate'. 'And I just adore my books,' she said to me. 'I have the Haj Raj, or is it the other way round? And Kaye's *Far Pavilions*, you know, the one based in Mount Kathmandu, well it's jus' the best travel book ah have found.' An open-plan kitchen led to a wall full of her collection; *501 Spanish Verbs*, *The Complete Bridge*, Stephen King's *The Shining*, Judith Krantz. 'I loved that English explorer Baker, and his wife, you know, the one he bought in Arabia. I just loved her big hats.'

Her gestures were as grand as herself. Arms outstretched and a head that posed in profile, suspended phaoronically like a Cleopatra. 'You know,' she said, 'you talk very even, regular voice, what's it called?' and she snapped her fingers and frowned, displaying a great feat of memory, 'Monotone, that's it. And if I listened to you for more than an hour I'd get bored.'

Not wishing to sentimentalise my own sense of worth, I reasoned that coming from her it was a compliment, infinitely better than the whiplash of her scorn. 'I want adventure in my travel reading. *The Far Pavilions* was wonderful and have you

heard of "The Haj"? Well now there's *The Raj*, all about India.'
I felt stuck for anything to say and asked her if she'd heard of
Chatwin or Mattiesson's *Snow Leopard*?

'They don't write so sensational a story,' I said, 'but they do
convey a scene beautifully.' She listened – she said she was a
good listener, but I suspected she was better at other things.

'Do you take milk?' she shouted from the other side of the
kitchen.

'Do you have any interest in the Bridges family?' I said.
'They settled not too far from here, I'm hoping to visit them.'

'Sugar?'

'Also the Welsh settlers at Puerto Madryn, only 174 arrived
to create a whole colony in Patagonia.'

'Is that so . . . tell me,' she said, handing me my coffee,
'do you like Morocco?'

'No,' I said. 'I had a heavy time in Tangiers and got stoned
in the Rif Valley.'

'I love it. I went for golf in Rabat and it was lux-sher-ey.
Unseen hands turned sprinklers on and off as you walked
around to play.' What a job I thought, crouched behind a bush
all day, switching a hose pipe on and off so this fat turkey
could keep the soles of her golf shoes supple. 'And the attach-
ments in the locker room were like in a palace. Gold taps and
more of those hands to lay out your bath towel whilst you
showered. I was alone and it was wild and you know, it only
cost two dollars so *anyone* could play.'

'Did you know that 70 per cent of the population of Tangiers
were without work,' I said, 'and that there was no unemploy-
ment benefit or pension scheme. Perhaps they might be more
prudent how they spent their two dollars.' She seemed
nonplussed.

'Listen, if they really want to work then I assure you there's
work to be done. We live in a *free* market, dear,' she said
with a certain quackery. Turning to her bookcase, 'Ah *Green
Mansions*,' she said. 'My favourite. You should read it and not
be too serious.'

'Is that the one like *Thorn Birds* but set in the Amazon,' I
said.

'Sure, and he had a really big house.'

'His wife ran a brothel you know.'

'Is that so,' and as she snapped her hands on thighs powerful enough to scrap an automobile, one did not need to be a
genius to realise that one's hour was up.

27

FIVE

I left Punta Arenas early the next morning. Enrique had, as promised, sent his driver to pick me up in a car large enough to live in. We were to drive to the airport to meet three German ladies from Santiago, and then be taken to a hotel built on an island in a lake made grey by the meltwater of a glacier. Sitting alone in the car while Juan made the connection, I idly thought of my only German phrase, '*Lagen sie sich ich denke das ich liebe sich.*'

There was a tap at the window. '*Guttentag*, do you speak German, we are going to sit in the back with you.' The promise of some fraulein, lean and wistful, perspiring and smelling of sweet decay made me slightly petulant as the most guttural and broad-beamed of old trunks squeezed into the car. On the long drive back to Puerto Natales, I could think only of their perfume, laid on so thickly it could have pickled an octopus.

Driving back along the road I had endured on my bike made me giddy with the distance covered. After lunching on the outskirts of Puerto Natales, we continued towards the base of the Andes. Before long, Juan told us that the hotel would soon be in sight. Amidst mountains that seemed to stretch to the heavens, and lakes that were as deep as the earth itself, my companions were snoring gently.

The hotel, Scandinavian in style, had timbered cabins with magnificent views. The Torres del Paine and sister mountain, Cuernos, were structured in granite and, when the clouds cleared, their tops were the colour of graphite, as sharp as a pencil. Three of the largest glaciers branching off the Patagonian icecap, Grey, Dickson and Zapata, fall straight down to the valleys now covered with lakes. For three days I was to luxuriate in comfort, being led by the hand like a doll, in turn, with each of the German ladies. How they took me to their bosom was not dissimilar to a train crashing into buffers, but somehow I survived. And miserable in my comfort I left.

28

The road to the edge of the park was no more than a day by car so I set out to walk until I got a lift. All morning I walked past gulches and *mesas*, a dried stream bed littered with dead trees, flanked wth golden thorn bushes and stubbly yellow grass growing out of flaky red mud. *Guanacos* stood and mooched before chasing each other up and down steep-sided slopes that formed the base of peaks so high that I was like an ant walking past a cathedral. Flinging myself off the road I slept through lunch, only to be seduced awake by the raven sound of a buff-coloured ibis.

In the distance the dust of a truck was getting closer and as it stopped near where I lay, the driver fingered me to the back without saying a word, his lips tight as a clamp. After an hour we reached a fork in the road where he stopped, waiting for me to climb off. He had the bottled-up look of a man who might one day commit a massacre and, not having spoken a word throughout the ride, he sped off. I carried on walking for a while, watching condors tease me from the summits around which they effortlessly flew. As the afternoon drifted towards evening I walked and sat, sifting the air without the wind in my ears in a rare moment of tranquillity.

Shovelling through a roadful of dust, a pick-up appeared from the opposite direction and pulled up in a cloud of dust.

'You wanna wait for the bus,' the driver said with an American accent. 'There's a bus a day and it went right on by just around lunchtime.' He paused to smile, 'And it's well gone past lunchtime and you sir have jus' bin asleep. But if you want coffee you can come by my camp if you like, it's only over the hill.' And, shaking me by the hand, he told me his name was Dick.

After fifteen minutes' drive we parked and walked down a gorse-covered slope. In the hollow of a valley, a lake sparkled with a late-afternoon sun. Not too close to the lake edge, a tight wall of square granite rocks was circled to frame a fire. Cans of powdered milk beside two tents and a washing line completed camp. 'Look,' Dick said, 'over there. My babies.' And he pointed to the left of the lake where some fifty *guanacos* loitered, bucking or nuzzling or, as Dick said, learning how to play.

'The *vega*'s looking quite good.' A strong, round-faced girl walked into the camp. 'I've done another good count, Dick, and the *guanacos* didn't even bother I was there.'

Dick introduced me to his friend, Fawn, and poured coffee from a black kettle. 'We've seen groups of 102 of these beasts and we're monitoring their behaviour to determine their eating habits by doing a *vega* count. And all we're doing there is analysing various grasses in different areas by weight and content and so work out their migration pattern. Somehow *guanacos* won't touch beautiful grassland and then you realise why. Trees and surrounding higher ground provide good cover for a puma to spring.'

While he was talking, he fingered a dark moustache and looked dreamily out of a face burnt red and dry by the sun. Picking up a bleached femur, he showed me the ball joint that had been chewed without mercy. 'Puma kill. Quick as a wink, break their neck and knaw 'em down to the ground.'

With the earnestness of an American faraway from home, Dick and his friend told me about their folks back in Kansas. How they had wanted a baby. The adoption fund had reached four thousand dollars for one of the cheapest but they'd spent it to come here because Dick hadn't been able to get a Fullbright scholarship. Fawn looked as if her body had sunk down to her legs which were already cumbersome and, in the inimitable Californian way, had been a computer programmer before becoming a traveller.

'Before this we used to light candles and listen to Neil Diamond,' she said languidly. 'Now we need them to see and the romanticism is all gone.' As I laid out my sleeping bag, lines of clouds dyed with ochre stood out against a polar blue sky. Dick handed me an adventure magazine called *Outside*, and the page that fell open contained a small stop press:

Three years after a meticulously planned and executed solo of Mount Hunter, John Waterman (at the time reportedly into hallucinogens) attempted to solo the east buttress of Mount McKinley to generate publicity for his campaign to be president of the United States. Setting out without tent, sleeping bag, or dark glasses and carrying little more than flour and margarine for food (to dramatize the plight of the world's starving) Waterman headed for a heavily crevassed section of the Ruth Glacier at the base of the mountain. He was never seen again.

SIX

On 28 November 1521, Ferdinand Magellan sailed past Cape Desire into a sea so tranquil he named it Mare Pacifico. He thought it was a sea because he could hear the roar of breakers hidden beyond the mountains. Such was the measure of value of the sixteenth-century spice trade, that Magellan's discovery of a passage through to the Moluccas, however appalling the loss of life on subsequent expeditions, was hailed as one of the greatest nautical feats ever. His eventual circumnavigation of the globe gave him that rare honour of being a legend in his own lifetime.

I looked out over the strait from the deck of the ferry *Melinka* at Tres Puntes near Punta Arenas. I was sailing across a stretch of water with so chilling a history that I felt like the pea on which the princess sat – insignificant, but not entirely so. By 1540, a total of twenty-one ships had been employed to find and sail through the strait. Twelve had been wrecked near or in these waters and of those that actually reached the Pacific, only one, Magellan's *Victoria*, had returned to Europe. Of the men who had tried to supply the spice-crazed merchants with their goods, 2,000 men perished and only 20 per cent had regained their cherished shores.

The crossing was cramped, with twelve of us stooped below deck, trying to sleep through the swell of the rolling sea. Clunking into a harbour made calm by a quay that stretched out to meet us, I wheeled my bike off the car deck on to a bitterly cold land of fire. Riding around the jetty towards Porvenir, a small Yugoslav settlement on the Chilean side of the island, I called into what looked like the only place in town to eat, the Yugoslav Club.

Fresh white tablecloths hung over small square tables around which stone-faced men sat alone, eating their food methodically. Pictures on the wall showed the warm Adriatic lap on the shores of Gorski Kotar and Kalnik, a strict reminder of how it could have been. The cold grey seaview through the window could not have been more forbidding. A cluster of houses perched on the opposite shore of a small inlet stood bleakly and hard. I ate a plateful of stew and potatoes, gurgling any remnants with a mouthful of tea. While it was obvious I was a stranger – and stranger still to come by bike – no-one appeared to notice my presence. In a land of emigrés I was just somebody else passing through. Cycling the length of the Andes has no place in the importance of life for such pragmatists. Stepping outside, I wheeled my bike into a wind that was blowing towards the Argentine border. The wind was strong enough to flap old newspapers down the main street and small children were in danger of being blown away. A little distance from town, low clouds looked mean and dark. If this was a truce between the sea and the sky then I was thankful.

Climbing out of town and away from the Strait I settled quickly into a rhythm. My style felt easy, a little swinging of the body but steady enough to support the pumping action of my legs. Feeling at ease with the journey, I allowed myself long deep draughts of cool air, ventilating myself, and for long periods afterwards I hardly seemed to breathe at all. At such times I felt like a hawk sitting on the wind, effortlessly keeping watch. Either side of the road, the sea of heather was purple. At each ruffle in the moss, there was a flapping of Patagonian geese. Buried deep within the heather, they sprung out in panic.

For the first hour, the road was good, surfaced and smooth, a dotted white line – a symbol of civility. After a while parts of the road had become broken and thin, exposing the heads of little stones, made greasy by the rain that was beginning to fall. Dried and wetted by the wind and rain, the knobbly stones were polished by eye-slitting grit, scratching at the surface. And as the wind became stronger there was the chance of my being thrown to the ground.

The road careered down to a coastline yelping with gulls. There were no sheltered coves here, no green-wooded glens, brightly flowering shrubs or clear calm streams. They were the stuff of dreams and balm to the senses of men who had paraded these waters in history. I was soaked in seaspray, cold to the core and numbed by the concentration needed to remain upright on the bike. Yet I was making progress on the birds. How rare it is to ride faster than the birds. And all the time I was watchful for stones that would slice into tyres, rip into inner-tubes, break rims or twist me into the gutter.

Looking south, towards Cape Horn, I could see only flat-lands of heather barricaded by a horizon of mountains that almost seemed unreachable. Unlike a desert where nature often seems immobile, such a still spirit appears too intangible to be real. Here, the wind is real enough. If it could do to me what it does to the trees, I would be ripped, denuded and spat out into the sky. Each time I fumbled around the promontory of another hill, blasts of wind pulled me to the earth, forcing me more and more to hunch over the handlebars. Dragged down to the speed of the geese that tried vainly to edge into the storm, I counted passing kilometres in the way that trees marked time.

On the frontier at San Sebastien, the formalities of transfer from country to country were about to begin. In one hut my passport was thumbed, stamped in another, customs forms were dispatched, completed, returned and someone wrote extra to the stamp, 'imported one bicycle' and 'Goodbye from Chile'. As I began to leave, a young guard said he had seen me in the paper and would I like to stay at his place for the night. His face was young and unlined, a square, honest face that jerked on his neck like the head of a chicken. He looked through my papers with quick movements that lent him a sense of authority. Yes and no was all he would say in English, and he smiled at his own sense of comedy. 'Yes, no,' and he looked up, still flicking the pages of the passport. That he could do two things at the same time, look at me and read inky scribble from tattered pages, was ample evidence of his genius.

He pointed through a small window to a group of wooden houses, standing defiantly on a broad crest of land that was but one simple settlement removed from some primordial beginning. I would have been happy to have anything separate me from such body-carving wind. So we walked across the heather, his jackboots creaking, to a house, laced with a garden fence within which a lawn, trimmed square, became, in its primness, a gesture against the relentless schedule of nature. And the wind clawed at me. Making it easier to breathe out than in, the buffeting wind hurriedly grabbed at everything else in the way, dragging in her midst a polar cold.

He unlocked his front door, and I left my bike outside. It would be irony indeed should it be stolen from a policeman's house. Inside, high ceilings covered bare wooden walls, adorned only by gas mantles which the guard duly lit. A green glow expanded to all but the darkest corners, making shadows fall across a littered table. Clearing the remnants of the previous meal, he quickly began to prepare something for dinner. '*Mía* wife, yes, no,' he said pointing towards Argentina. '*Mañana, ici* – she go for baby, she back tomorrow.' I helped with the salad and with the little wine that he said he had saved for a special occasion, he proclaimed this an honour. He sang '*Si Vas Para Chile*', and we ate and drank until I heard a clock chime twice. Juan was a guardian of duty employed by what many regard as a dictator. I was sure that didn't make Juan a dictator too.

The next morning I rose early. Juan had been obliged to return to work later that night, but his wife, now back from her travels, had arranged my breakfast. The radio spoke of more rain, but the direction of the wind would change in my favour. Checking once again that my panniers were securely fixed to my low-riders, I wheeled my bike along the garden path before stepping out into the wilderness.

It was 14km of rough road to the Argentinian frontier and the formalities were nothing more than businesslike. The impersonal daily routine of life goes on, war or no war. Nothing showed of the so-called enemy within except for a sign standing defiantly a few yards from the customs hut. It read, '*Las Malvinas son Argentinas*'.

12   Harberton, in the final stages of being settled. Now tourist maps and brochures produced . by Natalie will slowly generate an invasion.

13   Near the River Chubut, a river course that stretched from a hard-won civilisation through the land where one already existed.

14   *The road from Serena to Monte Grande parallelled the river in the Valley d'Elqui.*

15   *The road further into the Andes to El Colorado was not really a road. It was a stream bed which vehicles and bicycles sometimes used.*

16   Views of the Atacama Desert, which flowers twice in a lifetime.

17

18

19

_____SEVEN_____

The road south to Río Grande was unpaved, but wide and smooth from there to Estancia Viamonte. All day I rode heavily into a wind that had once again turned against me. Each circle of the pedals braced against the gale and the biting cold. In the distance I saw a cyclist being paced by a car and, should I catch him up, I too could take shelter in the slipstream. Slowly I ate into his lead, gasping deep lungfuls of air.

My heart pounded, enough for everything I saw to lose a little of its colour. After a full hour of being teased by another cyclist on a journey you naturally take to be your own, I was close enough to hear his breath. I was ready to pounce on to a calm quarter of car, to hide from a wind that was now blowing head on. One more push and I could heave to a position behind him and then ride alongside. I could smell embrocation on naked legs and sense through his desperate moves, the sway of shoulders, the nodding head, a level of urgency. It was as if he were determined not be caught. Ten yards more and I would be assured of a safe haven when suddenly the car began to slow. The cyclist indicated he was turning back the way he came. Damn. How I cursed his lack of consideration and my own stupidity for succumbing to such combative pride.

Overtaking the car I turned and smiled, wished him good day and pedalled briskly past. Looking back I saw the car U-turn and in view of no-one but the gulls I slumped, aching, on to the handlebars.

In the foreword of a book called *Of No Importance*, Rom Landau mentions the problems of the autobiographical text:

Most of us cherish imaginary romantic notions about ourselves and

*only rarely succeed in breaking through the crust of self-deception
. . . In books of an autobiographical background an occasional
word of self-criticism is usually outweighed by pages of self-praise,
however cunningly disguised.*

Lucas Bridges concluded that 'the truth contained in these
remarks has greatly delayed the production of my memoirs'.
The result of Bridges' memoirs was his definitive account of
life with the Indians of Tierra del Fuego, *The Uttermost Part of
the Earth*.

Describing the intrusions of Western man, Bridges would
have understood the meaning of Alan Moorehead's term 'the
Fatal Impact', even though it was being applied to the South
Seas. Growing up with Indian children, fearless with each
other as children tend to be, he showed no fear as a young
man, leading his party from Harberton to the northern Ona
lands and Viamonte. In the introduction to the book, Gavin
Young wrote of his having a 'strong, kindly character' and
describes how Tschiffeley wrote of his 'keen, sparkling eyes',
his 'powerful hand', the 'smile playing over his face'. Young
was right when he said that 'he reads like someone one would
have gone a long way to meet'.

A couple of hours later the road widened to the size of a
runway and as beautiful a stretch of road as I have found
anywhere in the world. Such smoothness allowed my jarred
limbs a few hundred yards grace when back on the track I
bumped along the Atlantic coast. In the distance I saw a set
of farm buildings which I assumed to be the Bridges family
home.

The house was shielded from the wind by tall conifers, and
it stood on one level. Entering the garden I wheeled my bike
towards the door and peered in through the window. A group
of people were seated for dinner around a table so polished it
reflected their faces. An elderly lady caught my shadow and
sent someone to the door. I explained that having read Lucas
Bridges's book, I had come this far to be here. 'Then you must
join us for dinner,' a tall fellow said in thickly accented English.
And leaning my bike against the front of the house, I went in.

Clarita Goodhall, seated at the head of the table, was a niece
to Lucas and had married a Goodhall, and it was her son

Adrian who had opened the door. His wife Stephanie sat opposite me and their son and daughter were further down. Clarita's brother Len sat to my right. Uncle Beetle was sat as far from Clarita as the table allowed. After I answered a few polite questions, little else that evening was expected of me and, with a matter-of-fact kindness, I was allowed to eat in silence – until, that is, Uncle Beetle buttonholed me during the sweet.

'Born in England I was,' Beetle said to me. I looked up. 'Knew someone called Lawrence, his plane landed in a tree. Got hung up there, great shame that, the ornithopter not getting off the ground.' The boy sniggered and Clarita continued eating as if nothing had been said. 'You know tumbler pigeons?' I shook my head. 'Well, if they close their wings they drop like an ornithopter. I remember seeing one do that. It went quite out of control and went and broke its neck.'

The meal was mutton from the farm and dessert was rice pudding. The simple welcome of this family had made it quite acceptable for me to arrive, if for no other reason than the enormous distance I had travelled on such an eccentric vehicle.

'From England by bicycle, by jove,' said Len, and he chuckled.

The family were retiring early that evening but I was invited to relax in the front room. Reseated in front of a pot-belly stove that stood as high as my chest, both Beetle and I were quiet. Beetle had been staring, possibly glaring, at me but it was impossible to know. Age had gathered itself around his face, folds of skin on a shrunken head that disguised easily what he may have been thinking. He clutched in his hand a silver torch.

'I have been bad with my nerves ever since the fire a couple of years ago, it affected me very badly.' Stirring only to light a cigarette, he sat in his chair, his body rummaging around for a comfortable position. 'I was born in Tonbridge, you know, in a house once owned by Henry the Eighth. The then owner had his head chopped off,' Beetle said close to glee. 'Well, that's what Kings were like in those days. If they didn't like you, off with your head.'

Beetle, with his dapper Louis beard and neatly kept moustache, kept his head slumped deep in between his shoulders and whenever he spoke, it sank deeper still. Beetle was quiet, his cigarette burning down to the quick of his nails. I waited for the conversation to continue, and in a smoky haze he opened his eyes.

'Me,' he said, 'I'm just fed up. I don't live, I just exist. I should like to put a bullet through my head but I don't have the courage.' As he coughed, the ash from his cigarette flaked on to his bone-dry hand and he jumped. How age crumbles the most virile of men, reducing them to powder and dust. 'I used to be crazy for that thing over there,' he said pointing to the television. 'What with all the video tapings and violence and *pornology* it disgusts me,' and he sighed. 'Do you remember Gracie Fields?'

I said I did.

'Well . . .

> "I wish I was a Casawary
> On the Plains of Timbuktu
> I could eat a missonary
> And his Himbuktu." '

And beginning to chuckle he started to cough himself into a stupor and, as if to placate his hell on earth, the old chap fell asleep.

The tide of evangelical fervour that engaged the first decades of the nineteenth century to establish the piety of the Victorian era, stretched as far as Tierra del Fuego. If Fitzroy was zealous in his dealing with local heathens, Allen Gardiner was a fanatic.

Born in 1794, Gardiner pioneered the idea of setting up a Protestant mission on Tierra del Fuego, which was eventually accomplished by Thomas Bridges. Joining his first ship at twenty, he later returned from action off Valparaiso bearing military honours as acting lieutenant. Travelling widely for the next eight years, he became increasingly religious. After marrying a wife with poor health (she had five children), he sailed, on the year of her death, to South Africa and set up the first mission station in Port Natal.

Journeys to New Guinea proved unsuccessful and for reasons of Catholic and tribal interests, Chile likewise was out of bounds. He decided to turn his attention to the wild aborigines of Tierra del Fuego. The Indian chief, Wissale, was predisposed to the building of a mission, so much so that Gardiner returned to England with all speed, and formed in 1844 the Patagonian Mission Society, whose headquarters were in Brighton.

A year later, he and an accomplice lay-preacher Robert Hunt returned to Tierra del Fuego and continued their dialogue with Wissale who now reversed his attitude and proved to be fractious and openly hostile. Once again they returned to England where bitter disappointment fuelled even more his quest to convert some part of South America to Christendom. Barely four months after being in England, Gardiner set sail with a Spanish Protestant, Gonzales, for Bolivia. On 5 February 1845 they reached Cobija (now in Chile) and two days later set off, riding and marching across the Atacama Desert.

During the next five months they covered more than a thousand miles, each man suffering terrible bouts of fever. The local tribes were unimpressed. However, a little luck blossomed and eventually they had an audience with the President of Bolivia, himself at odds with the Catholic Church, who agreed to their request to build a mission. Gardiner returned again to England, only to be notified that a change of government in Bolivia had reversed their decision to a resounding no.

Gardiner had striven with unbelievable faith, only to have all manner of circumstances try and twist his resolution. That we are left with a man incapable of anything less than his last role begins to become clear. Eleven months after his return from Bolivia, Gardiner, accompanied by a ship's carpenter and four sailors, set sail from Cardiff. When they arrived back at the southernmost tip of this great continent, they found a good site, well sheltered, with a plentiful supply of timber and wildfowl. The only problem that had to be resolved were the Fuegans. Their distaste for the foreigners was evident. Becoming daily more audacious, the natives placed the men in fear of their lives, so forcing them to return home again. On reaching England, Gardiner pronounced the need for a floating mission to cross this slough of despond.

Gardiner's tenacity was unquestionable and his courage unbreakable, but one wonders about the calamitous effect he might have had on such primitive people. Returning for the last time across a raging South Atlantic sea, transporting two launches on the *Ocean Queen*, he and six companions were set adrift in Banner Cove on 5 December 1850. Two 26ft launches were obviously unsuitable to house a mission and it could be that twelve years of futile endeavour could have unbalanced Gardiner's mind. His boats were undermanned and, when they made camp, predictably the natives resumed hostilities. Gardiner's plan was to sail through the Beagle Channel and find Jemmy Button, Fitzroy's young captive of sixteen years ago. Should that fail he would procure some boys from a tribe and enlist help with language and introductions to neighbouring tribes. How naive he must have been to think enemy tribes would listen to each other about a subject they neither cared about nor understood.

Further calamity was to strike with the realisation that they had left all of their powder and shot on the *Ocean Queen* and were therefore unable to shoot for their own food. On 24 January they moored their boats in Earnest Cove near the mouth of Cook's River. Malnutrition began to undermine the health of the party despite the purchase of fish from the Fuegans. It is possible Gardiner's accounts of hostility were less than reliable. A tribe of armed natives could surely overpower six weak and defenceless men.

As winter approached and the sea began to freeze, the end was drawing nigh. When their net was torn to shreds by ice, Gardiner simply said, 'thus the Lord has seen fit to render another means abortive, and doubtless to make His power more apparent, and to show that all our help is to come from Him'. Sadly, help did not come from *Him*. The first crew man died on 28 June and on 6 September Gardiner wrote the last entry in his diary and the tragedy was complete.

I was a guest at Viamonte for three days and enjoyed enormously the company, needing a rest from the bike. I particularly liked Clarita, so sound of spirit she and her brother Len were inseparable. She mentioned Uncle Lucas, remembering him as a child, gambling about all those years ago. 'It's all in the book,' she used to say, referring almost reverently to her uncle's masterpiece. 'Everything you need to know is in the book.'

In the early 1890s large areas of open pampas around here proved excellent for rearing sheep. To the Ona, sheep were just deliciously easy prey, a sort of woolly *guanaco*, and not to raid sheep on their own land was unthinkable.

Total extermination of the indigenous population was

thought by many white farmers to be the only line of defence and they began to employ hunters who were paid one pound sterling for every native they shot. With armed gold prospectors also blasting all and sundry in their pursuit of riches, the Ona were placed in a dangerous situation. So, complying with a request from the Ona to help them defend their northern territories from the onslaught of white men, the young Lucas decided to embark on an ambitious project.

After years of toil with his father and family at Harberton, he decided to create a neutral land-holding in the northern areas to allow the Ona some refuge against genocide. For anyone outside the family, it was a massive undertaking to cross forests full of Indians so skilled in the art of ambush that they had never been seen to attack. But in 1902, Lucas left his home with forty-two pack-horses carrying a ton of provisions and tools. With a young Welshman, Dan Prewth, he reached Najimishk four days later and built a one-roomed hut which they called Viamonte, and with such as they had, stayed for the next five years.

Now, the house is larger, but several outhouses still exist and a large sheep-shearing shed stands behind the main house. It was strange seeing the reality of something which in a book always takes on a feeling of fantasy. Viamonte and the understanding of the Ona tribe may have been a small historical enactment, but it was crucial to the development of Tierra del Fuego, and integral to my story. As the sun shined, I basked contentedly as Lucas Bridges must have done looking out over his ranch. After prolonged negotiation in Buenos Aires, he secured the title to 254,000 acres of land which, in 1910, supported 100,000 sheep and a stream saw mill imported from England. Even with this encouragement the inevitable could not be stemmed.

Towns that sprang up on the northern boundaries were like bright lights to a moth, and, attracted to such an alien environment, the Ona began to degenerate. Two epidemics of measles, brought from the towns, ravaged the land in 1924 and 1929, decimating three-quarters of the race.

Packing my panniers once again, I said goodbye to Clarita and Len. The rest of the family were busy on the farm except Beetle, who was asleep. When I heard the gate close behind me, the clasp chinking into place, I was back on the road. Before arriving at Viamonte I had ached for a comfy chair, while now I wanted to sit on my bike and pedal. It was as simple as that.

EIGHT

Pedalling gently with a wind pushing from the north, I eased into a bigger gear. So slow was my progress, the chain racheted on to a cog which until now had not been used.

The road to the end of the earth undulated through a forest of silver-trunked trees supporting the songs of its birdlife. Without the whistle of the wind in my head, Tierra del Fuego gave off other sounds. I could hear blackbirds rattle off a tune, backed up with the drumbeat of the woodpecker and the kwok-kwok of the grouse as occasional base. There are a hundred varieties that either live here or stay a while on their holidays: grebe, duck, woodpecker, widgeon, eagle, hawk, owl, gull, plover, swan and vulture; along with mountain, forest and sea birds such as grouse, swift, swallow, flamingo and wren. I had hoped to meet the Magallenic penguin, the Rockhopper with its Fu Manchu whiskers, or perhaps the Emperor himself. Instead of the spectacular steamer bird thumping its way into flight, I had the pleasure of accompanying the chirpy London sparrow.

I saw foxes scarper after rabbits, and plovers pecking at their worm. And, stretched out in the gutter, squashed woodpigeon marked out the miles. But, oh, where were the giants of Patagonia that I had read about in my youth!

Dreaming all morning, I climbed and descended small twists of the road; bumping and bashing along, creaking handlebars and brakes that squealed on downhill bends and sometimes in the distance, I thought I saw the sea. Instead, I squinted through bars of silver bark and the breathing of the forest of the giants; the centre of the universe where legend records they live. If the centre of the universe was here, then Kwonyipe was the giant.

Of all the Ona magicians, Kwonyipe was the most masterful. Great in wizardry, a dab hand in the parting of the waves, he was also in love. Legend tells of the Ona people having sustained a great massacre of their women and the inauguration of the lodge, which they called the Hain. Back to times far older than history, when the rain was filling the lakes and the sea still washing up new lands, the giants Kwonyipe and Chashkilchesh walked in the woods, their heads above the tree-tops. When Krren (the sun) and Kreeh (the moon) walked the earth as man and wife, and many of the sleeping mountains were people, only the women had the power of witchcraft. And if displeased, only they had the power to dispense ill-fortune and death.

Well, so the story goes – as passed on through the generations by the misogyny of men – the chaps were a bit cut up about this and conspired to kill off all the women. This left the Ona, in the centre of their universe, with only themselves to play with, as they waited impatiently for the little girls to grow up. To prevent future matriarchal ascendancy, they formed a secret society banning women from the Hain. Still fearful of the past, they fortified their position by inventing strange beings which lodge members would then impersonate to keep the frightened woman away.

Krren (the sun) followed the example of the men and intended to kill his wife Kreeh (the moon); the scratches appear as craters. She ran away up a mountain called Aklek Gooiyin and leaped from the peak, only to be followed by her husband; and there, above the faraway mountains made grey by the eagle, they raced on the horizon as sun and moon.

But something was stirring down below. Kwonyipe lived happily with his wife and son until one day he met the most enchanting of women. So strong was her allure, it had the power to cement stars to the sky. So bashful was she, that it was only possible for her to be wooed in the twilight. So with all his might, sorcery and magic, he became like a God and made the sun and the moon sink out of sight.

In the darkness they embraced. Her love, having been fought for with such dastardly brilliance, had been brought to a satisfactory conclusion. Ever after, the sun and moon rose and continued to circle the heavens, but not as before. Dipping sooner and rising later, the sun created shorter days, and, allowing Kwonyipe more time with his love, the moon bore longer nights.

Still twisting, still gripping the bend of the handlebars, I freewheeled down a short slope towards a small white-painted house, its red roof a beacon on the edge of a glade. Slowing down to stop I walked my bike and leaned it against a bridge roped from bank to bank. Crossing over a stream which washed the tears from a weeping willow, I stepped into a garden edged with roses, polyanthus and daffodil. So orderly was the form, the lawn bristled like fox fur, a veritable Garden of the Hesperides. A blonde-haired lady leaned out of the window and asked me if there was anything that I needed. I said I needed water, and she pointed to the stream and closed the window.

As I filled up my water bottles I saw from the corner of my eye, the girl walk across the lawn. She tapped me on the shoulder. 'Take these,' she said, handing me biscuits, nougat, some bread and three apples, and standing for a moment she then turned and ran back into the house.

There had been no opportunity to buy food all day and I hadn't wanted to ask the Bridges for more than they had already generously given. It was strange I should find this house at the very moment I'd wished to eat. Riding down the road, I ate my food by a lake, mesmerised by the shimmer of the giant's trees.

That evening I slept on the shore of Lake Fangani, and the next morning climbed up to the crest of a mountain. After an hour's hard riding, I reached the summit of a range that had plagued me since first sighting it from the plains. And turning to the lake, I stood where the Ona showed Lucas their northern land. The descent lasted almost to Ushuaia. It was fitting that I should drop from the mountains to the end of the earth.

At the bottom of the world I could hear Madonna. Music pouted out of the ether from radios strung to scaffolding overlooking the Beagle Channel, and unfinished buildings were growing in a boom-town culture. As I rode down streets which paralleled or went down to the sea, there was an energetic air of the frontier. People were busy on the street and trinket-keepers did a flourishing trade. Inflatable maps of Tierra del

Fuego dangled next to three-foot penguins waistcoasted in jackets that said 'I love the South Pole.' When in 1863, Lucus's father Thomas sailed into the channel after spending seven years on a treeless island in the Falklands, the reality was probably more exciting than the dream.

Shifting along a corridor with windows facing towards Cape Horn, I carried my bike into my hotel room. Being charged a pound for the night, it was not the Savoy, but, unbelievably, tucked away under long curtains, there stood another bike. On the lower bunk a Japanese fellow slept on the covers in his underpants, his tongue vacillating with every contorted snore. Sparsely furnished, the room had space for one more machine.

Stealthily abandoning my own, I seized the moment and vigorously tiptoed across to his. Sabotage was my first thought and then tie up the enemy. I felt like Sylvestor's arch-enemy the cat, and wondered if I should undo a screw. If I undid his quick-release bolt his front wheel would fall off when he next moved the bike, but it wouldn't have been funny for long. I felt strangely like a man self-exiled to an uninhabited land only to discover another form of life. When coming to my senses I decided everything was cool as long as we continued in different directions, impracticable perhaps in the most southerly town in the world surrounded on three sides by the sea.

Here, my life depended on the way I related to bicycles and the preparations I'd made for this journey. This bike sounded as if one pannier contained the contents of a whole cycle shop, and all I had were three spanners and a chainlink extractor. In specially fitted pockets, each of eight water bottles sloshed full with liquid as did a plastic drum fastened over a sleeping bag. The frame was small, at the head stem the crossbar met the downtube. Wrapped around the top of the rear stays beneath the saddle, was a black concertinaed rubber hose, concealing a moving part. Pushing down on the saddle the back of the bike appeared to be supported by springs. The straight handlebars, dressed with five mirrors each decorated with a plastic flower, outflanked a horn, sellotaped to the handlebar stem, and large enough to sound a battleship. Packed with six large panniers, the bike was too heavy to lift and had the presence

45

of a warhorse. The noise of my repositioning his machine woke up the man.

'Ah cyclist,' he said, his eyes still influenced by the vacancy of sleep, 'you have found cycle.' He paused. 'It is mighty beast. Ah, forgive me, haw pleasurable to be meeting you,' and standing, he quickly banged his head on the top bunk. 'Haw bwoody heller.' He rubbed his head, saying, 'Englishman teach me in Bowivia.' We shook hands and he gave a short bow. 'My name is Kyosai, it is short name for long name which mean "Two Crow on Flowering Plum in Winter". My father, he had strange sense of humour. And please, your name?'

'Nicholas,' I said, 'it means someone without any underpants on.'

'Ah yes, I understand, same sense of humour,' and he laughed. 'You like cycle?'

'It's a bit heavy.'

'Velly necessarallily to be so. I am tortoise.' And humping his back he walked slowly around the room.

'Why are you here?'

'Same you. Long voyaging. Forever away.' A blast of cold air blowing in through the open window made him shiver. Reaching for his clothes hung on the corner of the bunk, he dressed before unzipping a front pannier and pulled out a thick leather jacket. 'Beautiful eh? Flom E-qa-dor. Velly cheap.'

'Very heavy to carry,' I said.

'Much important for cold.'

'S'pose you were desperate for food you could always eat it.'

'What! Eat jacket. Not understand.'

'Indians around here would often eat their own rawhide moccasins if the winter was too harsh to find food.'

'Ah yes. Interwesting adwice. Thankyou.'

He was short and swarthy with wispy hair around his chin. Looking around the room he muttered to himself in Japanese, over and over again. Quickly I unpacked a sweater and replaced my cycling shorts with a pair of jeans. I was ready. After five minutes I asked him what he was saying.

'What I say?'

'Yes. Have you lost something?'

'Ah, yes.'

'Shall we eat?'

Eventually we stepped out of the room and into the corridor.

Leading to the stairs, it opened into half a dozen rooms. In each a clutch of radios was tuned with the same predictable lyrics. Boys slicked back their hair, preening themselves as they mouthed what sounded like someone misbehaving with a microphone. They slapped their hips as we walked past and the Japanese cyclist bowed to them all and walked quietly on.

Next door to the hotel was a restaurant specialising in seafood. He wanted to eat there, where a waiter guided us to a table.

'Each day, eat here. Same table, same chair, same food, same wine.'

'Don't you get bored?'

'No. I am dreaming.' He was a strange elixir of man, every night ordering a bowl of giant mussels. Steaming and in large slate shells, he said they reminded him of his girlfriend. A red wine was brought to the table and he poured us both a drink, gulping his own before I'd reached my glass. The evening continued with wine being consumed at a ratio of three to one.

'Which route did you take to get here?' I asked, hoping he may have a few tips for my return haul.

'Buenos Aires by boat to here, Japan to Buenos Aires with aeroplane.'

Drinking one more glass of wine, he momentarily became silent. 'Sartre once say, that choice is possible and what not possible is *not* to choose. I can always choose. But I must know if *not* choose, I still choosing, yes?' I nodded. 'So I choose here to be with cycle, and tomorrow I make new choose.' I asked him if he studied philosophy. 'Yes, but it no good unless you want. Here I want. Your English philosopher Mr Russell say once, that you must go to Poles. That you must climb high mountains . . .?'

'No choice?'

'Ah, solly . . . must *be able* to climb mountains *if want*, and if space journey passes, that too.' Kyosai's outlandishness reminded me of something that I'd read from Bertand Russell: 'I get a great deal of literature advocating that if only I took their drugs my hair would turn black again. I'm not sure that I should like that, because I find that the whiter my hair becomes, the more ready people are to believe what I say.'

NINE

In September 1884 four ships from the Argentine Navy arrived to establish a sub-prefecture at Ushuaia. Three weeks after they arrived, the Indians were dying faster than graves could be dug. Measles were to the natives what the 'plague' was to seventeenth-century England. Those who survived barely had the strength to dump their dead outside the wigwam. Others managed a burial of sorts underneath a bush.

After the Keppel Island massacre where an aptly named Captain Fell and a party of men were clubbed to death for no apparent reason by Fuegans, the founders of the mission, Reverend Packenham Despard and the Reverend Stirling, returned to the Patagonian Mission Society in Brighton, disillusioned men.

Despard's adopted son, Thomas Bridges, begged to stay in Argentina and this he was allowed to do. Eventually, at the age of twenty-five, he returned to England to take his Holy Orders. In a whirlwind romance he married Mary Varder in her Devon home of Harberton, from where, two days later on 9 August 1869 they sailed for the Falklands, reaching Keppel Island in the October. In August 1871 their preparations to journey to Ushuaia were about to court disaster. After eight days' battling against a westerly gale they sighted Cape San Diego, the easternmost point of Tierra del Fuego. It took the next four weeks for the 88 ton schooner to battle through the ferocious riptide of the Strait of Le Maire, involuntarily being shunted back and forth through one of the most hazardous channels in the world. As they docked, Mary clung to her husband's arm and whispered, 'Dearest, you have brought me to this country, and here I must remain; for I can never, never face that voyage again.'

By 1876 the settlement of Ushuaia had grown to the size of a small village. Four British families had taken residence and over one hundred Yahgans broke with their nomadic lifestyle.

20   Typical house in Magallena, Chile. Estancia Penitentes symbolised the ultimate conquest of many a pioneer.

21   Mr Gwyn Rees in his garden in Gaiman, Patagonia. (I suspect he spent most of his life in Patagonia perfecting such an array of splendour.)

22   *The road from Serena to Monte Grande. This valley was made famous by the people simply for being there, as recorded by Gabriela Mistral.*

23   *View of Monte Grande.*

Abbreviated from the word Yahgashagalumoala meaning 'People of the Mountain Valley Channel', Yahgans differed from the Ona mostly through habitat. The Ona were the 'forest men' the Yahgans hunted and lived in canoes, vessels that Captain Drake's chaplain thought 'the most exquisitely constructed little craft in existence'. They sat in a frame of split saplings, sheathed in strips of nothofagus bark, sewn together with whalebone needles and animal sinew. Small fires were set on beds of sand to keep the hunters warm. On shore the Yahgan hunter could kill a sitting duck from two hundred yards with a pebble thrown with unbelievable accuracy.

But then the navy arrived and eight years later most of these native Indians would be dead. The Mission Society would listen to nothing that Bridges had to say on the formation of a reserve protecting natives from the influx of white men. That, he was told, was not his evangelical business. That the natives were strangers to repetitive toil, free from drudgery, and had access to a variety of daily tasks which demanded a high degree of cunning and self government, was not taken by the mission to be sufficient to uphold human contentment. Such was the zeal of early evangelists. The debacle of damnation awaited them if they defied the will of the Lord.

At the time it was estimated that the Yahgan population numbered 3,000. Before the memory of the navy had vanished, there were 300. The total population of Yahgan, Alacaluf and Ona tribes was around 7–9,000; after a hundred years of Christian domination by men trying to alleviate the suffering of the 'sad and tragic savages' there is not a convert alive today to thank them; the indigenous population of Tierra del Fuego is extinct.

Bridges broke away from the mission and set up a ranch forty miles east of Ushuaia. Extending along fourteen miles of the north coast and inland to the base of the first range of hills, about six miles, the farm included twelve off-shore islands. The buildings themselves were built at the head of a deep gulf allowing for the anchorage of quite large craft. This brave new settlement was called Harberton, after Mary Bridges' home village, which it would take me most of a day to reach. Twenty miles out of Ushuaia a sign directed me to Harberton.

A right turning led through a glade of grey and reedy trees.

The road narrowed and sloped into a semi-darkness of thickly shifting branches, phrasing the shadow through the leaves like an etching, placing the journey into a tunnel. Cutting through the zebra shading made the air twitch and my eyes began to flicker. Adrenalin was surfing in my arteries, deep breaths feeding a racing heart; airy thoughts hypnotised by the trees. It was uncanny the ease with which I could pedal, odd how little I needed to steer. So sublime, so fluid did I feel on the bike just then, it was as if I were floating along a road cooled by the moistness of a brook in the glen.

The brushing of the bike in the wind sent a rabbit fleeting, hurling its bonny ears through a prickly hedge. Clumps of daffodils grew yellow as a submarine, and poppies kissed in the breeze. And the scent of pine from the needles and cones, watered by a brook which babbled, was deliciously perfumed. Peeling away in the rising morning the shadows kicked away the shackles of half light, beginning their escape from the trees. Stripped of shadows the trees moved back and the stream washed away the stippling. The glen widened around a homestead and a man who was shouting in the forest.

His pigs were running loose, squeaking and squirting, battering into matchstick fencing enclosing a run-down shack. He was shouting to me as I cycled past.

'Me peegs,' he yelled pointing at my bike. Shrieking down the road they lunged into open space as far from the bike as their curly tails could push them. Cloaked in hair that fell to a chestful of beard, the man scowling, marched over to me, breathing heavily. 'Me peegs, what you do with peegs?'

'Nice peegs,' I said.

'Bloody tourist,' he said in English. 'Speak English huh?'

I nodded.

'All day take to find me peegs, and you scare shit out of 'em all and onto me house . . . look, everywhere.' Pig splatter steamed all over the road.

'Where did you learn English?' I asked.

'Same place you, bin England in war then went crazy then came here. I live in me house twenty year.' He paused to fumble in pockets tailored from hessian. 'Damn, gone run out like me peegs. You got bacco?' No tobacco, no wine, nothing to share with this old man.

'I've an orange . . .'

'Can't smoke orange, you stupid. What you say I smoke grass and fly after peegs, ah, yes here,' and holding up a screw of tobacco, he rubbed it into a clay pipe plucked from his hat. Waiting a moment to savour the pleasure, he looked benignly at the scattered pigs that he knew had nowhere else to go. Lighting his pipe he breathed in a lungful of twist and said he felt better. 'Ya, ya, that is nice you know, the sun shine, wind cool and you know I have names for me peegs, but sometime they all look same, ha . . . ya go,' he said with a raised gesture that could have been directed to pig or me, 'and next time call to peegs nice things and they not run away.' He walked away chortling, having exacted a toll of sorts. His pigs were the guardians of his patch.

And then, from the trees to the hermit and around the corner to the smell of cooking meat, it was strange. Picnicking, a family hailed me to them, occupying my hands with beef and wine. The father clasped me warmly, proclaiming that people should never become divided by the countries on which they stand.

Further on I turned towards the crest of a small hill which held unwrenchable roots of a silver tree shaped by the force of Antarctic gales, and denuded as an old man's hand: like a tree of life that had been there forever. So down and down I cycled, settlement in the distance, a rutted farm road skirting around the waters of the Beagle Channel, rumpity-rump at the bottom of the world.

When Thomas Bridges decided to move from Ushuaia to Harberton they scoured the area they knew as Downeast. The first site they considered was soon replaced by a second, judged more suitable, but in calling that Thoughtof, they followed the Yahgan way of names.

The eventual plot, known to the local tribes as Ukatush, was renamed Harberton; the house was built on the site of an ancient Indian village, the Yaghan name for it was Tuwujlum-biwaia (Black Heron Harbour). It was here that Bridges began to compile his life's work, the *Yahgan-English Dictionary*. Charles Darwin's belief that the Fuegans were cannibals related in part to his knowledge of their language. Listening to them talk gave him the impression they repeated themselves, and he estimated that all Yahgan speech was derived from around one hundred words.

Such simple people, he believed, were the missing link

51

between civilised man and the primates and would surely eat their own kind. If language is a judge of man then Darwin could not have been more wrong. Bridges' dictionary contained more than 32,000 words and inflections. His son Lucas recorded how they might be expressed:

> the Yahgans had, at the very least, five names for 'snow.' For 'beach' they had even more depending on a variety of factors: the position of the beach in relation to that of the speaker, the direction in which it faced, whether the speaker had land or water between it and himself – and so on.

Words varied according to the position of the speaker – the word for a canoe would be different according to whether you were in the canoe or standing on the shore. 'Among the variations of the verb "to bite",' Lucas continued, 'was a single word that meant, "coming together on a hard substance when eating something soft," such as a pearl in a mussel.'

I stayed only a few hours at the farm. Natalie, the American wife of Clarita's son Tommy, would talk to me only if I subscribed to her charity and my three pound daily budget would not be worth her breath. Tommy was quiet and bearded with a mane of greying hair wizened at the edges. He had a long-suffering countenance when he wasn't flying his plane, which legend tells of him flying into a tree. He smiled when I mentioned Uncle Beetle.

'I've only got 920 hours but that was over four thousand landings. It's all gone now, lock, stock and barrel – engine checks in Bahia Blanca made it too expensive.'

We were quiet for a moment, then I said that I had to head north, across Tierra del Fuego, to the next stage of my journey, to Patagonia.

Looking back at the Beagle Channel I quietly said goodbye and then turned inland, towards Harberton and Flat Top Mountain and the river Varela that dropped to the sea. Back on the track home, I would have to face the peegs. When the old man saw me coming, he ran into his house slamming shut the door, and the peegs dropped their load with a vengeance.

For a week I churned across Tierra del Fuego, the beat of the wind hammering on my back. Each day the same. Asleep with the sun, I awoke as it rose, with heather in my hair. I was out of my bag and back on the bike still harbouring the tail-end of my last dream. Back the way I came, Viamonte, Estancia Pampa, across the River Ewan, and San Sebastien.

And so the road worsened, tarmac being replaced by pebbles and stones, and barely stretching the width of a truck. Ahead, a jet-stream of dust signified signs of life. Trucks in convoy plastered me with their comet's tail that turned my face to the colour of earth.

All day I counted the miles, only to forget how many. The days, too, blended into one diurnal event and, if I squinted across the plains, I could think myself somewhere else. Rumble-rumble, the bike and me, jingle-jangle across the plains. Onwards to the mighty Strait once more where the eastern edge meets the confluence of the Lomas, where the ferry tramps daily between Punta Espora and Punta Delgada, where an 800-mile ride along the coast of Santa Cruz will always haunt me.

TEN

On 31 May 1520, Hernando de Magellanes anchored his ship to winter in a small bay on the eastern side of South America. The ship's diarist Francisco Pigafetta, who survived the first circumnavigation of the world, christened the region 'Patagones' or big feet, after discovering large tracks treaded by the giant moccasins worn by indigenous Indians. It was thought to be a land of giants. Legend tells of a magical kingdom hidden deep in the plains for the brave and the few to find. The kingdom was believed to have extended between the Cordilleras of the Andes and the Atlantic Ocean, and to have descended from the Río Coloraro down to Tierra del Fuego. This is Patagonia, in secret.

Thirteen miles up the Chubut Valley, the small town of Trelew is situated a little south of parallel 43 degrees. It had taken me a week of the most monotonous cycling to get there. How the pedals seemed heavy, how hopelessly drab had been this edge of Santa Cruz.

The Chubut Valley is a huge area of 140,429 square miles, the third largest province in Argentina, making up around eight per cent of the land area and situated in Central Patagonia. To the west the Andes contained the valley as did the Atlantic Ocean to the east. South was the Province of Santa Cruz and the Río Negro to the north. The name Chubut was originally Chupat and is the Indian name of the river meaning tortuous or sinuous. Local Indians called the river plain Chupat but the similar sounding word *shupar* means in Castellano 'blind drunk'. Yet drink was not what made the area attractive to prospective settlers.

The river was of greater use. Rising in the Cordilleras of Río Negro Province, it winds down over 600 miles until it reaches the Atlantic near Rawson where it traverses large areas of pampa *mesetas* which are unnavigable and infertile. Only in the last 40 miles has the area been transformed into what has been called the 'Desert and the Dream'.

A pretty red-brick chapel on Avenue Belgrano, inscribed 1889, was hidden away in the city and locked. Trelew was no longer a Welsh town. In the old days there would have been neither sanitation nor public water supply and, like its neighbour Rawson, 'its nocturnal silence riven by the howls of wild dogs who scavenged in the badly fenced cemetery' contrasted with the day when 'noisy beats of runaway horses or cattle escaping from the corrals in the midst of scattered houses was like a small cattle town in the far west of the United States'. The Touring Club Hotel on Avenue Fontana had, I was told, a feel of the old days. Nearer the centre of town I asked for its whereabouts and came across a recurring problem – communication.

'I . . .' and the fellow I asked paused. 'I . . . don't speak the English.' About to ask someone else, he touched my shoulder.

Beginning with a pause which was filled with even greater effort he said plainly, 'It es difficult.' He stopped speaking and so I asked again, becoming absurdly irritated at his weak grasp of English.

'Directione a Fontana?'

'Ah sí,' he said. 'Gracias.'

'Directione?' I was breathing impatiently, tired, truculent . . .

'No.' His eyes were close together and he looked in pain. His pink tracksuit was soiled and ragged and his gaze had become distant. 'I have book, much book English,' he said, 'but . . .' he paused again and as if the struggle to talk had become one of mass internal conflict, he stood up, shrugged his shoulders and walked away. I felt sorry that I had allowed my fatigue to make me feel so unreasonable. I was in a better position than the settlers when confronting the Indians or the bureaucrats in Buenos Aires.

The hotel I found by chance. Leaning my bike against the window, I made for a place in the room where I could sit and keep a watchful eye through the window at the same time. All around the room, brown and grey tiles decorated the interior of the public bar to chest height above which a mirror travelled from corner to corner, seemingly to magnify the room.

Seated at a small round table, I asked the waiter to take my order for coffee. Occasionally brushing the large front window, the branches of a weeping tree rustled in the wind, speckling an old man with the shadows of its leaves. Slouched in a white whicker basket chair and wearing a white crumpled jacket, he was napping. Half-closing my eyes, I began to see Patagonia as I had hoped it would be; steaming with guachos, sheep, Butch Cassidy and the Sundance Kid.

It was as if all my life I had been standing in a railway station, imagining what the train would look like, disappointed when the train didn't arrive on time, and incomprehending when it didn't arrive at all. This must have been the fear, multiplied a hundred times, of every brave pioneer that stepped ashore off the little ship *Mimosa*.

The *Mimosa* was a clipper destined to carry 150 Welsh people from the land of their fathers to a mysterious clime. A mixture of family groups, single men and middle-aged leaders were drawn in almost equal numbers from the heavily industrialised county of Glamorgan, from the Mountain Ash and Aberdare areas, and from rural North Wales. A few of them came from Liverpool and Manchester where the Welsh took advantage of the work offered in the cotton mills, and among the passengers there was one North American. Leaving Liverpool on 25 May 1865, with the incongruous and sad refrain of 'God Save the Queen' echoing around the docks, the pioneers set sail on a journey that ranked with the *Mayflower*.

Yet the ship had never ventured south-westerly with trade winds before, particularly such as these, blowing them far below the equator and into the South Atlantic. Argentine admiration for these people had in the beginning been high: Juan Hilarian Lanzi, an Argentine commentator, describes them as 'standing with arms aloft, engulfed in the emotional farewells of parents and friends and with fond adieux on their lips and tears in their eyes – the Welsh epic and the miracle of its adaptation to Argentine conditions had begun at the moment of these fond farewells'.

The *Mimosa* finally anchored in New Bay on 27 July 1865 at a point near caves where the women and children were forced to take refuge. The rough seas of midwinter made disembarkation difficult, taking eight days to complete. The feast of the landing is still celebrated on 28 July.

Shoeshine boys carried their wooden boxes stuffed to the brim with rags and polish. My canvas shoes were unpolishable but still they came. Stacks of bottles lined the bar. And outside, hailstones began to pummel the streets while a wind whipped clouds in between the speckled shadows and the sun. I felt lethargic, transfixed in time, bound by tradition. I felt loyal to the sweet polish of the bar, the clattering of waiters, the hum of café traffic channelled to this or that table, and the faces that become expectant and then sanguine. I was expecting the Welsh valleys here to be modelled on a rural Merthyr Tydfil with donkeys clunking coal from a handmade pit. I would soon have to come to terms with my ignorance. All afternoon I sat in that bar, reflecting on why I should journey so far to be here. It was simple enough when Tarkovsky said 'that we live, have our ups and downs and we hope. We lose hope, we die. And we have to start from scratch again.' It's not an original thought but during an adventure it's a patient one, and recurs often.

Gaiman, 12 miles from Trelew, was supposed to be the most Welsh of all the towns in the valley. I rode out of Trelew on a wide stretch of road that would eventually be the track that would lead me across Patagonia to the Andes. Cycling along a slip road I freewheeled off the ridge that harboured the road into Gaiman. As quiet as a siesta, the main street was bereft of life, except for the unmistakable sound of dominoes being clacked through café windows, to reverberate in the still summer heat. Off the main street stood a house, painted white with a wall-size Welsh rose emblazened next to a dragon. The words Casa de te Gaiman were the sign that I had begun to get closer to the Welshness that I'd been looking for.

Inside the house, Welcome to Wales teatowels had been pinned on the wall along with all the artifacts that might grace a café anywhere on the coast of the home country. Scones and tea were served to me and a coachload of tourists from nearby Puerto Madryn gave off the sounds of Rhyll on a sticky day.

Through a mutual acquaintance I was introduced to the Gonzales family. Mrs Gonzales was at first cautious then enthusiastic about my arrival in the town. She poured me tea and gave me a large slice of fruit cake which she had baked herself. Crammed into a rambling old house, itself perched in a forested hillside overlooking Gaiman, Welsh tables and dressers vied for space with a collection of antiquities that stretched back three lifetimes to the beginning, to the cargo hold of the *Mimosa*.

'We had Bruce Chatwin here you know,' Mrs Gonzales said, her Welsh voice lilting like a song. 'He spent many hours around you know and then he went and wrote unkindly,' she paused, as if I too might collude with Chatwin. 'To entertain, I suppose.'

If she was a dominant force in the family Mr Gonzales was gentler. Slender and quiet, he wore half-moon glasses and peered kindly over the rim. He loved the music of Carlos Gardel who died fifty years ago in an air crash over Columbia.

'He sings better every day, even though he died so long ago,' he said. 'In the Carlos Gardel era there was more optimism after the crises in the 30s and Gardel was uplifting.'

'Let's not talk about politics, Daddy, the green beans are frozen.' Mrs Gonzales flustered into the room nervously.

'I think he should know,' he said without force, but with a charming sparkle in his eye, disguised only when he was at pains to mount his glasses. 'You should read Graham Roberts Cunningham, he buried Tshiffeley you know, after leading the cortège with his horses.'

Favio, their son, came in to sit down. He was about eighteen and having discontinued his studies that week was not in good favour. 'I should be sitting for my exams, but you know, I won't go. There are other things that I want to do.' A call from the kitchen shouted us to a table steaming with roast beef, new potatoes, sprouts, carrots and a boatful of hot rich gravy. Grace was said and when I asked if they were celebrating anything, Favio said that they ate like this every Sunday. So it was Sunday! Before I tucked into the meal, I thought it was Friday.

ELEVEN

Immigrants are the unsung heroes of Latin American history. Less prolific in taming vast tracks of wilderness than their North American counterparts, nevertheless they undeniably conquered the land here. When 30 million people emigrated to the United States between 1800 and 1930, only 7–9 million went to Latin America. In 1865 153 pioneers came here and another 112 in 1867. North America offered clearer opportunities for the land-hungry European poor: landowners in many Latin American countries already had Indian and African labour which was cheaper than any imported workforce.

It was only during the last quarter of the nineteenth century that the Argentine government realised the benefits of immigrants and grasped how their willingness to open up new land could be exploited. Yet they were still ambivalent. Most of the privileges of citizenship were given generously whilst allowing immigrants to remain under the protection of their country's consul.

In the United States, naturalisation was a prerequisite for voting so political parties had an incentive to coerce new people into the fold. Dictatorial governments do not need the votes. Welcomed for racial reasons 'that they may whiten the stock', North Europeans in particular were actively encouraged. But their politics, perniciously democratic, were distrusted. Germans founded the first Argentine socialist party, Italians led the first labour unions in São Paulo and Spaniards introduced anarchist ideas into Buenos Aires.

Third generation families like the Gonzales supposedly have no barriers to political ambition, and yet Mr Gonzales was worried. 'We have a governor, Nestor Perl. He is a Jew and advocates open divorce and we are a Catholic country. No-one has been so open before and I just wonder what will happen. If he is too open, I assure you he will be replaced by someone who is not, and nationalism is not good for our valley.'

The next day, an introduction had been made for me to visit Gywn Rees. He and his wife owned one of the tea houses in town. Mrs Rees brought in a pot of tea and a cream tart – Teisen Hufan – which she said was simply egg white, sugar and vanilla essence cooked in the oven for half an hour. With the texture of cheesecake and mouth-wateringly creamy, it was delicious.

'I once went to Wales in 1955,' Gwyn began, his back to a row of Welsh dolls that stood on the mantlepiece, 'and then only for a few days.'

Dotted around the room, were sepia-tinted photographs of unsmiling faces. An upright piano gathered a little dust. Nearby hung a photograph of the main square of Ruthin, the clock tower casting a shadow over a café in which I had drunk tea for years.

'The language is getting lost these past hundred years and in twenty-five years it will be all over.' Gywn was accepting this fate. A culture must adapt if it is not to die. 'Now we gradually turn into Spanish. Even the Eistedfodd is partly Spanish,' he said, sitting back in his chair. 'We are very well looked after by the custodians of Argentina you know. But why not? We are after all one of the most peaceful settlements in the world. You know, we lived with the Indians for nineteen years before the conquest of the desert.'

I mentioned that Glyn Williams, an author and TV presenter in Wales, once said of the Welsh from Patagonia that, if they retired to the old country, their mixture of Spanish and Welsh, could not be understood.

'That's a lie,' Gwyn shouted, 'it's modern Wales that has changed, not us. And it is the language that comes off worse, getting more and more obsolete.' He showed me a dictionary where nearly half the words, marked with an asterisk, demoted them to literary oblivion. 'Five hundred years before the birth of Christ, there were twenty-four rules to write poetry. The gathering of Bards now say seven.' His disgust was academic, but then here, so far from the Bards, what else could it be?

Outside, the sun was warm. Down the wide main street, you could see everywhere the civilising influence of man, the broad pavements separating shop fronts from the drains. All I had to concern myself with was the efficient working of my bike. That the panniers were securely strapped and that I had enough to eat and drink was enough. I leant my bike against a simple one-storey red-brick cottage set back in a side street where it faced the sun.

'The only reason for not leaving your door open and unlocked is the mosquitos.' A man I took to be Mr Nightingale walked to where I stood on his garden path, fingering keys into his front door. 'Have you had any breakfast?' I declined his offer and sat down in his front room while he prepared his own. Switching on the radio at 3380 megahertz, he said, would get us news from the Falklands. Around his room which was simple and austere, the BBC World Service's *London Calling* magazine was scattered.

'I get free copies from a lady in B.A.,' he said, his eyes twinkling. 'Are you sure you don't want anything?' he enquired, cutting chunks of bread from his loaf. His life circled around a routine. Born in Tanzania in 1930 from British stock, he stayed and farmed until leaving for the UK in 1966. After working as a farm labourer in Lewes, Peterborough and Fotheringham, he took his family to the Falklands, where he lost his wife to another man.

'We had three children, free milk and veg, good salary and a nice house. But these things happen and I needed a change, so I came over here.' His duties as a municipal gardener were interrupted for breakfast, during which he switched on the radio and cut his bread every day in much the same way.

His features were certainly those of a farmer: solid, weathered face, sweeping grey hair across a high forehead, and large, strong hands. The broadcast crackled and Radio Australia suddenly drowned out the Falklands and, before he had time to retune it, had flipped again, this time to Radio Peking.

Ever since I'd read Bruce Chatwin's book *In Patagonia*, I had wanted to cycle across that great land. When I heard of his death – from Chinese bone marrow disease at the age of forty-nine – I felt as bereaved as if I'd known him, so infectious was his writing. He had wanted to visit Patagonia because of an obsession with a scrap of brontosaurus skin in his grand-mother's living room.

His grandmother's cousin Charley Milward was the captain of a merchant ship that sunk in the mouth of the Straits of Magellan. Milward survived the wreck to settle in Punta Arenas, discovering at the bottom of a glacier the perfect remains of a brontosaurus. This prehistoric mammal had fallen into a glacier and travelled down to the bottom of a mountain encased in a frozen river of ice.

Salting and packing it in barrels, Charley sent it to the Natural History Museum in South Kensington where it arrived a putrified mess having been gorged by the tropics. That scrap of prehistory belonging to Chatwin's grandmother was the only survivor, apart from the bones.

Anticipating a wind that would blow against me from the west, I knew my only chance to cross the plains of Patagonia would be to begin each day at first light. I blew it. Having overslept on the morning of my departure, I used up what was left drinking coffee with Mr Gonzales. When I stepped out of the house, the sun had already wound up a breeze. I would have to wrestle the bike forward until either sunset or the strength of the wind forced me to stop. In this land of the giants the elements can be out of all proportion to expectation.

I rode hard, pressing with a spurt of energy that had become restless for the road. Life on the road inspired in me a revolt. I was striking into an unknown land, thinking that a hairline across these deep southern wastes was doing more than just guiding me across a country. I expected too much. If a reason for this journey had to exist, then it was ideas that the crisp clean air made possible. Holding on to the possible was another matter. Standing with the bike in the vastness, where rolling *meseta* scrub can be seen stretching to all corners of the plain, my thoughts fluctuated from the reasonable to the ridiculous.

To be in all probability the only cyclist on a thousand-mile stretch of road would mean nothing to anyone but a cyclist. But before me there had passed many. Had the Indians not discovered their land before Magellan and he before the settlers? And how many cyclists, I wondered, had pedalled with the same euphoria that made them feel at ease with their fate?

By mid-afternoon I did not feel so cocksure. The wind was now hurling at me grains of earth, scratching into my arms, legs and face. Instead of concentrating on what I was doing, I knew from past rides that I had to let go and release myself from the toil. That, by concentrating thoughts away from muscles that pumped and ached, by a process of some systematic mechanical dehumanisation, they would not ache at all. This had always been the plan.

At times like this, the scrub, trees and unforgettable Patagonian landscape would be, in the face of such effort, sensed more than they would be seen. The smell of tarmac would overpower always the scent of *meseta*, except when the sun is not so hot.

Hour after hour I pedalled. Turning the chainset speedily I urged the wretched bike on. I was on the edge of one of the vast plains of the world, a speck of humanity cycling towards some faraway horizon from where I would appear as a flea on a dog's back. All morning I endeavoured to create a rhythm which could be maintained; at best, a trancelike thought process that didn't buckle in the wind. But, by late afternoon my legs were still aching. The rhythm that was to make me like an animal gliding around its habitat broke down in the face of a wind that conspired to grind all cyclists to a halt. In a fit of madness I rolled across the plain, thinking to catch and retain some Arcadian stag when I know it's not in sight. I decided to rest when a battered red bus rattled past, klaxoning like a duck.

_____TWELVE_____

Tschiffeley, the great horseman of the 1930s who rode 10,000 miles through the Americas to Washington, hated the car from the beginning of the trip to the end. If all his wishes had been carried out, 'Hades would be well supplied with motors and motorists.' And yet, as I watched the bus bludgeon on, I had to agree with the man himself, that 'being only human, I must confess that while driving about in a comfortable car I hold other views about them'.

I could see the bus pull off the road. It took fifteen minutes for me to reach where this heap of ragged tin stood, wisps of radiator steaming from its front. By the bonnet, under a blanket strung across four poles, two men were eating in the shade. 'Ah ah, at last, you are here, we asked ourselves how fast your legs would be,' a cheery face laughed.

'Eat?' the swarthy one of the two said, handing me a chicken leg. I thanked him and sat on the road edge.

'Water, eh?' said the older man wearing a neatly cut moustache, 'drink much eh, drink lots and lots in sun.' He paused and then offered me an orange.

'No thanks,' I said and asked if he wanted some tinned sardines I'd not eaten for lunch.

It was pleasant to be sheltered from the wind. At last I could hear. Brown gleaners, head down in the manner of tits, sat on their bushes and sang. Sedentary on the topmost twig, a red-breasted plant-cutter bleated its faint call, wailing its way from bush to bush in a series of jerks. The old man also heard the call.

'It is a nice bird, eh? I seen it all my life from when I was so small,' and he raised his hand to the level of his knee. 'But I prefer the tree-creeper, the plumage is softer brown, like the earth, and its voice is so high. But as you see, here we have no trees.' Looking around at land that was free for the audacious and worked by the brave, he turned again to me. 'Tell me, what are you,' he asked, 'French, German?'

'English.'

'*Inglaterra?*' He looked surprised.

There was a silence. The *guerra dos Malvinas* was still a sad and painful memory for Argentina. The old man tensed as two women came to the door of the bus. At first they said nothing untl the younger one hastily returned inside.

'Tea?' The old man beckoned me to sit down. There was an air of unease as he leaned forward on his stool, 'and what do you think of Argentina?'

I told him that I liked Argentina. I told him this because it seemed important to him, and just then it coincided wth the truth.

'That is good,' he said, nodding approvingly. 'And where else have you been?'

'Chile,' I said. Again the old man went quiet.

'And do you like Chile?'

'It is a very beautiful country.'

'But not as much as ours, eh?' he said with half a smile.

There was a pause as an elderly woman passed me tea. Sipping from the mug, I lowered my eyes from their gaze. For a moment, mingling with the birdsong, I heard someone sobbing inside the bus. I looked up, into the eyes of the old man.

'Los Malvinas,' he said quietly and sadly. 'Her son has not yet come back.'

The pampas seemed endless. An occasional ripple in the landscape was scant compensation for the Andes. As I rode on, shadows of the bike lengthening across the road, it was easy to imagine that the world was flat. Not far away was Las Plumas, a small settlement on the banks of the Chubut. A beer sign hung over the door of a large low barn so I went in and asked if they had any accommodation for the night. A young girl led me to the back of the barn, where hidden from view was a courtyard. She pointed me to a door across the way. I pushed the bike across the courtyard and leaned it against the room. The air, still as a summer's day, made the walls hazy.

I sat down next to the bike. A child's burbling carried between bowls of geraniums standing sentry at a door surrounded by smoky black pans. Ivy, the hunting ground of the gecko, hung like tassles down the far wall. Suddenly, with the gait of computer afterbirth, two of these eccentric beasts came out to browse. They strode like loose-fitting machine bits, from out of the shadows. And there, tucking into the end of the day, they charged their batteries with a last batch of sunlight before closing down for the night.

My room was in the corner furthest from the barn and next to the toilet. Furnishings were simple: a bed and chair smelling of wax and burnt wick and a view of the road stretching back to Gaiman. Lying on the bed I began to doze. It had been a long day and the blisters on my hands were glowing. The toilet was getting busy which meant the barn had started to serve drinks . . . had it ever stopped? When the system flushed it complemented the sound of intestines having a panic attack. On the verge of sleep, another load of stomach filtered into my senses and I thought of Pigafetta's giants. After an hour I was so stiff that I couldn't move. It was a Patagonian paralysis. As I drifted off to sleep to the sound of mobile debris boxes shifting their contents, I vowed in my next life never again to be a cyclist, a human or a giant. Falling asleep without getting undressed, I lay on the bed in my stink.

Inevitably, my inconveniences paled compared with those of Magellan. A Portuguese navigator in the service of Spain, he commanded an expedition of five ships that in September 1519 set sail for the Moluccas by way of a passage to the west. As well as raging seas and despicable weather he had to contend with a mutiny, the loss of men, ships and provisions, and the onset of scurvy. More than that, when they reached Port St Julian, on the coast of Patagonia, Antonio Pigafetta, the ship's fanciful diarist, wrote the following account:

One day, without anyone expecting it, we saw a giant, who was on the shore of the sea, quite naked, and was dancing and leaping and singing, and whilst singing he put the sand and dust on his head . . . He was so tall that the tallest of us only came up to his waist; however he was well built. He had a large face, painted red all round, and his eyes also were painted yellow around them, and he had two hearts painted on his cheeks: he had but little hair on his head, and it was painted white. When he was brought before the captain he was clothed with the skin of a certain beast, which skin was skilfully sewed. This beast has its head and ears the size of a mule, and the neck and body of the fashion of a camel, the legs of a deer, and the tail like that of a horse, and it neighs like a horse.

Not wanting the truth to spoil his chances in the court, it was fair to say that the imagination of Magellan's little chronicler had no bounds. He must have overdosed on some cerebral eye-poke when he made an entry in his diary describing a cure for the stomach-ache of a giant:

When these giants have a stomach-ache, instead of taking medicine they put down their throats an arrow about two feet long; then they vomit a green bile mixed with blood: and the reason why they throw up this green matter is because they sometimes eat thistles. . . . Two giants that we had in the ship ate a large basketful of biscuit, and rats without skinning them, and they drank half a bucket of water at each time.

Darwin was also mesmerised by the plains of Patagonia. Near the end of his narrative of the voyage of the *Beagle* he wrote:

In calling up images of the past, I find the plains of Patagonia frequently cross before my eyes; yet these plains are pronounced by all to be most wretched and useless. They are characterised only by negative possessions; without habitations, without water, without trees, without mountains, they support only a few dwarf plants. Why, then – and the case is not peculiar to myself – have these arid wastes taken so firm possession of my mind?

When they returned home, talk spilled in the clubs and the bars, of this 'land of giants' with a green Atlantis-like Trapalanda and its spirit-guarded lake on whose margins rose the battlements of a mystical city. There Tschiffeley could graze his horses in heaven's happy ground, alongside Caesar's eight-footed steed Pascasas and Bucephalus. Here was a land that was truly a myth. It was as glittering to the imagination as the great Manoa, which Alonzo Pizarro and Orellana failed to find. News indeed to heat the blood of any hearty explorer who could afford to go.

In a section of her book *Across Patagonia*, Lady Florence Dixie asks of herself, less obliquely than Fitzroy or Darwin, why she journeyed there, accompanied by Lord Queensbury, Lord James Douglas, her two brothers and a friend Mr Beerbohm. She says:

> *Many of my readers have doubtless felt the dissatisfaction with oneself, and everyone else, that comes over one at times in the midst of the pleasures of life; when one wearies of the shallow artificiality of modern existence; when what was once excitement has become so no longer, and a longing grows up within one to taste a more vigorous emotion than that afforded by the monotonous round of society's so-called 'pleasures'.*

How trying it must have been for Lady Dixie.

THIRTEEN

Waking before sunrise, I had only to get on my bike. Steadying myself against the bed, I then rode out of the room. It was 112 miles to Paso de Indios, and for seventy of them my feet didn't touch the floor. It was a game I played to endure the boredom, and having been blessed when I woke to find shoes on my feet, knew it was going to be a good day. The headwind was strong, and it would blow until the sun went down. But today was a gala day and I was like a fly on a coach-wheel, seeing what dust I could make. As if by magic I had travelled no distance at all. Looking up I could see Paso de Indios.

Paso de Indios was one of the centres of the Tehuelche Indians. A centre of trade dealing, among other things, in horses, skins, meat, foodstuffs and the local brew, *chi-chi*. In a gorge walled by cliffs of ancient sediment through which the River Chubut flows, the locals would have spent the days bolasing *guanacos* and chasing ostrich while the women gathered wood for the evening fire.

It's easy to forget that here, Indians are the indigenous people until governments wipe them out. The naturalist Wallace shuddered to hear a Portugese official boasting that he had wiped out whole tribes north of the Río Negro by dropping the clothing of smallpox victims on their land. In a manner of speaking the same happened here. Between 1832 and 1835, Juan de Rosas, a federal leader with strong ranching connections, relinquished his governorship of the Buenos Aires province to raise a military campaign against the Indians, pushing them further from the good grazing land and the traditional home of the nomadic Araucanians.

The wars of 1879–83, generally known as the 'campaign of

the desert', virtually wiped out the natives from the Pampa just a little north of here. Their effect filtered down, compounded by the arrival of European immigrants and later the new techniques: the agricultural machinery, barbed wire, well-drilling machines and hand-pumps, railways and roads, and ocean-going steamships. The exploitation of Indians' ancestral rights was inevitable. The proportion of Indians to 'whites' in Argentina is 1½ per cent, the lowest ethnic profile in all of South America.

As I rode into a town, most of it centred around the bar, I heard the sound of someone singing and men drinking, and then I realised the voice belonged to Placido Domingo. Above half-opened bottles of wine, a television set had been suspended by a rope attached to a hook in the ceiling. With the power of a baying ox the maestro lurched from one end of the stage to the other. Whenever he hit a high note, the sun-wrinkled cowboys glanced up to see if he'd split his gut.

I went over to the bar and, over the backs of broad-rimmed hats with men sitting elbow to elbow, ordered a drink. In the States these guys would have been called rednecks . . . to some, the antithesis of reasonable man.

'A beautiful singer,' I said, starting up a conversation with a square jawed rancher.

'He ees mag-nee-ficent,' he said, his Latin moustache dappled with beer.

'Shame he's so fat,' I said unthinkingly.

'No, no, that is ees 'eart that is singing. He 'as the 'eart of a bull.'

I'd begun to pick up a few words in Spanish and enjoyed stringing them together. Listening to people on the road, a guttural flow became noticeable, detaching words and reforming them. So without inhibition I started talking to everyone.

'Do you understand Italian?'

The cowboy shrugged his shoulders and lifted a jug of beer to his lips. 'Maybe after this I understand.'

I waited a moment, noticing how odd I looked in my black, stretch-fabric cycling shorts and peaked cap, coloured blue and banana-yellow.

'So where are you from,' he sniggered, looking me up and

down, 'escaped from a circus?' A couple of other men giggled into their mugs.

'Yes, a flea circus actually,' I said. 'No bath for ten days.'

'I bath with sheep,' he said bettering me.

'He likes the sheep this one,' someone excitedly said across the bar. '*Bastardo*, Miguel. You pig lover.' Turning to me, 'If they were hungry, they would eat their own mothers.' Rough as hard ground, and in a place where few travellers stop, their curiosity would keep you alive.

'But if he wasn't so fat,' I said, rejoining the conversation, 'then his wife would be able to embrace him.' The rancher looked around at me and stared as I gibbered a form of Spanish. After taking another draught from his jug he looked at the television.

'Maybe Señora Domingo has very long arms.'

The next morning, on the road to Tencke, I stopped for a while to watch a flock of ducks bathe. Against the blue of a lake fenced in by bullrushes, their beaks were deep orange and savage, and wild enough to wrench away a finger. Sitting passively at the water's edge, two pink flamingoes plucked grubs from their feathers. The sun was hot and further down the valley the road was cut into the side of the gorge, a classical arrangement of river and rock.

The ducks had given me a good idea. Pedalling to the point nearest to where the Chubut flowed, I leaned the bike against the crash-barrier and climbed over. Pulling off my tee-shirt I sat by the river, dipping in my toe. The river swirled past, twenty yards across but shallow enough to stand in. Peeling off my shorts, I saw a rock pool sheltered from the current and I jumped. The splash sent a shiver to my heart and, with the eyeline of a frog, I watched this desert river skim to the next meander.

Bright and fresh I fell asleep by the river's edge only to wake drunkenly later in the day. I was too relaxed to climb back on to the road and watched instead the flight of the flamingoes. Flapping against the sky, they lifted themselves slowly. Vigorously their wing beat became even and only a wing-span apart they flew as if attached by a silver thread of lake that from paunchy pink undercarriages dangled before falling back to earth.

Dizzy with the sun I dressed, remounted my bike and took a few deep breaths of afternoon air to vent my sleep. My tee-shirt, soaked in the river, quenched my burning back, water dribbling down the inside of warm thighs to leave a trail on the road. In the heart of Patagonia it was beginning to get hot. I steamed where I stood and as the sun evaporated the river from my body it was as if I were melting.

In the absence of traffic, and protected from the wind by the gorge, I heard a single songbird. Warbling like a thrush it sounded melancholic, alone in the valley. Pensive and mysterious at the top of its *meseta* bush, it simply intensified the solitude. For the rest of the day I pedalled in the valley. The road had inclined to Paso and would now sink to the heavy base of the Andes, three days west from here. I chased the shadows of clouds that formed a fleeting shade on the plain and watched little animals run the gauntlet across the road. As the surface began to cool, lizards raced to the white line, rushing across the hot spot as if it were freshly baked pipeclay.

Animal life is abundant in Patagonia. At intervals of less than a mile, furry beasts had been flattened by the wheels of some truck; bloody form scrunched from every orifice. Near a road like this where truckdrivers keep score of their kill, all the animals know that not to move is a sure sign of death. Either side of me, *nandus*, like the kangaroo, scattered like escapees, jammed along a road hemmed in like a bowling alley by *estancia* fences. Cars they understood but bicycles were altogether less predictable. As lorries chased the cars and cars chased me, I howled like a jackal and sometimes chased the *nandus*.

As each day became hotter than the one before, I slept under stars that reminded me of the Sahara. So clear was the air and so dark the sidereal sky, starlight took on the energy of cosmic synapses, bridging small gaps in the universe.

Under raging lines of black clouds I eased away from Patagonia. Slowly curving north I pedalled with a masterly wind the 90 miles to Esquel. Briefly I stopped for provisions, stuffing luxuries into my panniers that put a sparkle into a featureless diet. Patagonia had finally been crossed. A towering thunder cloud, which shaped in the wind and placed by chance, accompanied me on my journey. Each night when such clouds are illuminated by light from the moon my dreams are long, uninterrupted and unmemorable. This night was to prove an exception.

Bumping along an unmade road, still in the process of being surfaced, I made slow progress. The old road carried the traffic, but here, hedged in by two caterpillar lines of piled-up earth, I was on the bedrock of a highway. As the day slipped into night I rolled out my sleeping bag, and then sat down with the food I'd purchased in town. Milk tastes sweet in a dry mouth. The pâté, coarse and wrapped in layers of cooked ham, was wedged in a saddlebag-size hunk of bread. The creamcake was magic; the strawberry tarts a delight. My soiled tins of sardines could now be given to another traveller in need. Drawing the bag up to my neck I lay cocooned and slept.

'Get up! Get up! You getting up or is it we build round you or we make you all very flat!'

I sat upright as if in a spasm. A fellow in overalls arched over me holding a mug of tea.

'Drink this eh?'

I rubbed the sleep from my eyes and gasped at the size of the earthmover that had crept to within a bike-length of knuckling me through its rotary masher. While the workers enjoyed their impromptu break I drank the tea, packed my bag and then, after saying goodbye, scooted into the distance like a brainless rabbit scudding through the pebbles. Further on, a firmer track edged round a sweeping curve of heather where spring water tumbled down deep nicks corrugating the route. Today, the very air was frisky. Blustery and innocent, the wind brushed across the track scattering eddies of dust.

By afternoon I joined another highway that went down and down into an Andean valley of timbered houses and overhanging eves. Down past mountains grey and so lofty they pricked the black sky to make the clouds rain. Hungry and sore I stopped at a truckstop where three cowboys guzzled bottles of beer. So carefree did they seem, I imagined their faces unable to conceal an untruth and, if what they were drinking was really an unraveller of mysteries, I decided to have a bottle myself. As I climbed back on to my bike one of them came up to me.

Smiling black gaps in his teeth, he said, 'You know, I ride my horse, I watch my fences, I drive my dogs, I keep my sheep. The patron pays me and I drink my beer and sleep.'

Swinging down, more down, wheels spinning crazy and

whoosh then up and through and up, the pedals spinning, then, slow, slow-moving legs begin to pump and slow, down to the valley floor and straight and level then twist to El Bolsen. It was not very far once again to the base of the big mountains.

San Carlos de Bariloche is a ski resort on the shore of Lake Nahuel Huapi. This, the 'lake district' of Argentina, was dimpled with towering, snow-clad peaks. Punched through the forested *cordillera* sat stately Cerro Tronador. As deep as it was high because of the placidity of the lake waters, it was only half as high as I was yet to climb. So pedalling through a summer's day, subdued here to spring, I wove through a forest, an emblem of beauty on the mountains like a brooch.

After tasting the coffee in the pretty flowered Villa La Angostura I began to climb the lower slopes of the Andes on my last day in Argentina. The air was cool and I was brisk on the bike. Resting at a lower summit I munched an apple and sipped icy mountain water. The climb wasn't hard, but the road, circulating through the Paso de Puyehue, was as rocky as an old stream bed. A white Mercedes jeep was parked on the side of the road where a group of people were chatting. They called me over and asked me from where I came.

I described Glossop as being close to Manchester and the man wearing reflecting sunglasses said he knew the city well.

'I've spent several weeks in Manchester,' he said. 'I'm a paediatrition in Buenos Aires and you have an excellent reputation. But what interests me,' he continued quickly, 'is if you have experienced any problems in Argentina?'

'There was a slight problem with someone yesterday,' I said. 'He blamed the Malvinas and Picton Isles situation on me personally.'

'Ah yes, a nationalist,' he said quite unsurprised. 'We have a lot of those in our country. I tell you we have enough problems with our economy to worry about islands in the middle of nowhere.'

I suggested that Mrs Thatcher's retaliation had unwittingly hastened Argentina's return to democracy.

'Yes. It is true. Had we won the war, the military would have been in power for two thousand years. This is our history, the Golden Rule which is very simple. It is this, that he who has the gold has the rule. All the worker wants is money for food and clothes. He doesn't care about democracy, it is only the intellectuals who concern themselves with such things.'

He offered me a drink of orange and then wished the rest of my stay here pleasant. Returning to his car he switched on an engine that rumbled with the power of the city and quickly sped away.

FOURTEEN

From Osorno to Santiago the journey continued north for 600 miles. Undulating, the black tarmac of the Pan-American highway crazy-paved to the horizon like a crack in the earth's crust. Before journeying north through Temuco and the Mapuche lands, Los Angeles, Chillan, Talca, Curico and again through the heartland of Chile, I cycled to Valdivia to visit people I'd met in Villa de Angostura. For a weekend they strove to.adjust me politically.

He was a university professor who had seen scores of students battened by the police. His son took me to a nearby slum area on the edge of town. Chorrillos looked like a transient settlement on the poor side of Africa. It was recognisable by the smell of sanitation that muddied the main street. It was also evident that we were not welcome. Battle-grey wooden fences wrapped in barbed wire were the most obvious line of defence against intruders. The stance of youths loitering by alley corners suggested other methods of protection could be offered. By the doorways, girls stood and stared; pregnant, possibly from their fathers, they looked dishevelled and hopeless.

'Before you can begin to have a democracy you have to have human rights,' my friend said. 'Here they get nineteen dollars a month and a beer costs fifty cents. The rest they get by stealing or prostitution or both. Here it is like Africa.'

We walked back towards Valdivia to watch a rock concert by Congresso. Famous for their freedom of expression, their music, performed before three thousand fans, reminded me of Sting's *Nothing Like the Sun* album.

During the break in songs my friend quoted statistics: 'This year, TVs are 30 per cent cheaper so poor people can afford them and so watch the government's commercials . . . before, 1½ per cent of the GNP was spent on 8 universities, now it is

8 per cent for 23 universities which, educationally, are mostly at a lower level.'

When I told him that Chile's problems were not an isolated case, he looked surprised. I told him that children run away to London and have no constitutional right to income support. That they too have to survive by selling themselves to pimps and paedophiles. That as much as 9 per cent of the population own 84 per cent of the wealth. I told him that Chile was no different to anywhere else and suffered only from its inability to sophisticate its brutality.

That afternoon I sat with my bike by the river in the midst of marketeers and fish-heads. I was depressed by what I had seen and had become nostalgic and lonely. Where was L? How did she look? I thought of Dad, imagining him making yet another table. I knew only when the cycling stopped, so did I. When the pedals stopped turning I moved a little closer to the edge. My eyes were baggy, weary and glazed, my skin as tough as a brontosaurus's kneepad. I needed a rest.

Nearby the 'chin-chin' men danced for the crowd, banging drums on their backs while swinging into a whirling dervish. Sitting next to me, a man sat down and sighed. I'd noticed him carrying a tray of plastic pots which the kids bought to blow bubbles. Another youngster ventured forward and offered him some *pesos* for one of his magic pots. He obliged, showing him how to coat the ladel with soap and then blow through the hole. He was the bubble man who sold bubbles to children.

'What a job,' he said turning to me when for a moment we were alone. 'You know, I have travelled in many places as a sailor and now I am selling bubbles,' he laughed. With bushy eyebrows overhanging a cheery face, he laughed in such a way as to make it part of whatever he had to say. He was laughing now and said, 'When I went to seek my fortune I imagined many things. Artifacts of great beauty, people of great power, places as wonderful as dreams. But now, all I want to do is sit in the afternoon and browse in the sun and blow bubbles into the air for the children to catch. What is the use of all this travelling?'

I followed a red line on my map that led me full circle to Santiago, 500 miles from Valdivia and five days back on the road; back with the trucks and the pizza stops and the beer and the hookers in the lay-bys and there was I as firm as a dragonfly fighting a breeze.

For three days I lounged in the swimming pool of Bob's back garden. I had met Bob on my journey to Ojos del Salado the previous year, and he offered me sanctuary in Santiago. By the end of the third day I began to feel sick. I was nervous. For one of the few times in my life I conceded to fear. It was a needless exhibition of sentiment but there was nothing I could do to temper the trepidation. Chile was not dangerous for me, and neither was Ecuador or Peru. The Atacama Desert was similar in principle to any of the other deserts that I've crossed. The conditions in the Nubia or Sahara were considerably more debilitating.

But I was no longer able always to make a decision that could be trusted. I was sometimes fearful, not specifically of ambush or being hit by a truck, just fearful. So there, alone, I festered. I knew also that there are times when no one person can soothe your misgivings, when no amount of coaxing can ease the spirit into gear. Halfway through the journey I felt that I had done as much as I was able and cycled as far as I'd wanted.

I had always resolved never to give in unless on the verge of death. Yet such an idea was bound by a contradiction; that, assuming there is nothing reasonable about death's knock, how could I resolve to avoid it by reason alone, giving in *just* before it should happen. Aeschylus was killed by a tortoise, dropped on his head by an eagle. As the eagle approached, Aeschylus was on the verge of death, but didn't know it; so what hope was there for me? I decided it was perhaps safer to continue, never to acknowledge your fear, never to accept how close you are to having a tortoise dropped on your head.

Slowly I packed my front panniers tight, discarding the rear bags containing warm clothes. Bike spares and camera, passport, notebook, money, a spare jersey and shorts were all I should need for the rest of the summer. After hosing mud from the Andes, the bike at least looked clean, if it no longer sparkled. I convinced myself that I was ready to go, but in my heart I dreaded the move, the continual and eternal rolling from one mile to the next, one more village further on and a thousand unknown faces in between. The street to me was like a briar patch, but looking through the window at the raging bushes, just then it seemed particularly monstrous. Did Tschiffeley ever doubt? Did any of them? And if they didn't, why did I?

Wheeling my bike to the garden gate I said goodbye to Juan. His friends in Arica would be kind and let me rest after the desert crossing. Arica was 1,325 miles from Santiago. Riding away from Puerto de Valdivia to turn left on to a road that eventually swept in a long curve by the River Mopoche, both river and road raging through the city, I left Las Condas. Down a long boulevard passing eight bridges which crossed the river, I was shaded by tall conifers of the Parque Forestal before heading north and away from the city.

Soon I was on a road I knew well; having once before journeyed to Los Andes on an ill-fated expedition to the mountain Aconcagua. At 22,848ft it is one of the three highest peaks in the Andes. Cycling along the rich Aconcagua Valley, with her fertile soil and lush vines, reminded me of the journey. I had wanted to cycle to the highest point on earth that a bicycle could go, an absurd quest that had gnawed at me through the winter of 1986. When I reached Los Andes I asked an old man on a park bench if he thought it was possible to ride to the summit of this mountain. He said I should have to be a goat, and a mad goat, but he wished me well.

I remember the valley climbing into the Cordillera, winding along the river Aconcagua for 21 miles until it reached the village of Río Blanca and the confluence of two rivers, the Blanco and the Juncal. As I chased a string of cyclists towards the Argentine border, the route to Caracoles and Mendoza, a huge transcontinental train chased me, until at 4,300ft, the height of Río Blanco, it could go no higher. I remember catching the cyclists and saw only their horrified faces when I related my quest.

Leading me to an army barracks they translated specialist information from a mountain regiment who advised against the climb on account of the deteriorating weather. I asked if they knew of another climb with a gentle enough slope for a bicycle and they suggested Ojos del Salado near Copiapo, 550 miles from Santiago.

It was 48 miles to Los Andes from Santiago and cycling along this valley was one of the most beautiful rides I have ever known. It compared with the road to Pokhara in the Naubise valley of Kathmandu, it was as godlike in its beauty as the downside of the Appalachians before reaching the banks of the Susquehanna. Here, the vines hung lush in a sun that, at day's end, sits on the crest of snow-capped mountains which recede into the evening haze.

Old men sitting outside cottages, drinking wine, shouting and laughing to their neighbours, passed around the bottle. The women unwrapped their headscarves to allow hair, like dripping tar, to cool in the onset of night, striations of broom-sweep following their path. Kitchen stoves began to fire, echoing the smell of dinner in smoke that permeated through still air. And, listing under a weight of wires on trees roughly disguised as telegraph poles, the air was humming with a lament as sorrowful as any plucked from an old piano.

Entering the outskirts of the small town, more and more wires began to lace together both sides of the road. What was left of the blue sky could be seen through the strings of a harp.

On that previous visit I stayed in the Hotel Continental, where simple rooms overhung a cavernous interior like a balcony. I collapsed into bed, hot from the sun, tired from resting in Santiago. Dozing into and out of thoughts of home I consciously snapped the shackles of nostalgia and thought no more of my sadness. After dressing and washing I stepped into a street teeming with gaily clothed youngsters.

Pulling myself onto a stool in a bar full of men, I sat quiet for perhaps half an hour when someone tapped me on the shoulder.

'Are yoo Englesh?' It was a Scottish accent and I turned to

24   *A view of a desert which flowers twice in a lifetime.*

25   *Licancabur Volcano, Atacama is probably the most symmetrically shaped volcano anywhere.*

26   *Uru Indians at Lake Titicaca.*

27   *Cuzco by night. Yes, my camera takes fancy pictures when positioned on a wall at f/8 for two seconds.*

face a young fellow with short curly black hair. 'Tha' name's Alan, I saw ya come into town, can I buy ya a drink?'

I accepted his offer and we began to talk.

'So what do yer think of Chile?'

'Easy travelling,' I said. 'Not at all what I'd expected.'

'Yer probably thought yer'd see riots everywhere and police in full battle-dress, eh?'

'Only what I read in the papers.'

'Oh, it does happen, but not like tha'. I mean, have yoo seen any trouble while yer'v bin here?'

Not a single baton had been slung.

'Nor, yoo won't see anythin'. Think of it this way . . .' He paused. 'Another drink?' I bought him one. 'Yoo knaw yoo hear of someone from the government gettin' kidnapped, yea? And tha government blames tha Left? Well tha Left then blames tha government, claiming it's a plot to undermine their cause. I mean can yer imagine it, tha government kidnapping their own . . .' He slurped another pisco and laughed. 'Well, I can, it happens all tha time.'

'What about the Left, what happens with them?' I asked.

'Ach well, just about tha same thing. Someone from the Left disappears and they blame the government who in turn say it's the Left trying to discredit the Right. Last week a policeman was found dead tryin' to blow up a church in tha style of tha Left. A week later, a student was accidently killed tryin' ta do tha same thing.'

Pausing to slug back another glassful, he looked glazed. 'I tell yoo, yer best out of it. It's a Chilean matter and I don't think anyone knows what is really happenin'. After all, would yoo expect a Chilean cyclist ridin' around Britain to talk all tha' time about Mrs Thatcher?' I shuddered at the thought.

Just then he turned round to watch a woman walk in, wearing blood red lips, high shoes and a skirt that attempted to descend from her waist. 'Ah, she's a savage one tha' one. Ah say . . . do yoo wanna a woman, 'cos if ya do, a night wi' her and yud never be tha' same agin.'

'Supposed to be someone waiting back home,' I said with uncharacteristic meekness.

'Ah, I dunna wanna sound cynical, but I hope she's there when yer get back. I once left my woman furra week, and when I got back she was sittin' on a black man and couldn't even remember ma name.' He waved to the girl and she came over. 'Come her yer ravishin' creature,' he said, putting his hand to the top of her thighs. 'Ah, by tha way, ah,' he turned to me, 'bein' a Catholic country ah, an yer have ta be careful yoo 'ah dunna have any ah, yer know, a couple of "Johnnies" about yer person . . . ? No, I dunna s'pose ya would. Well then, what tha hell and, cheerio, it's been a pleasure.'

And grabbing the girl by the waist, he left me to slump in my beer.

FIFTEEN

There were certain objectives that I had in mind on this section of the journey; to visit the grave of Nobel Laureate Gabriela Mistral, journey into the interior of the Atacama to the oasis of San Pedro, and complete the desert crossing without losing, as one says, one's marbles. La Serena was halfway between Santiago and Copiapo, a four-day ride to the Valley d'Elqui where Mistral spent much of her early life.

After a good night's sleep I woke like a bird, but with a headache. I left the town and descended to the highway, half a day's ride away. Turning right at the Pan-American intersection I closed down all sensitive thoughts for fear of losing them to the lunchtime traffic. Inching my way towards the coast, the wind was sometimes behind me, sometimes blowing across from the sea. But all the time the wind was strong, bouncing off rolling Pacific breakers, each one bigger than the last until the final wave crashed with the perfunctory mighty roar to start the sequence again.

The further away from the city, the more sparse the traffic became, until, for half an hour at a time, I had the world's longest highway to myself. It was strange that I hadn't seen more cyclists. I expected them to be wheeling their way down from the north, rotting and dazed, obliterated and crazed by the desert. But I was once again alone. At the end of each day I ate in a truck-stop by the side of the road, slept by the sea, mesmerised by the night-time lapping of the Pacific.

After passing through Los Vilos, Illapel and Ovalle I reached Coquimbo, and on the beginning of the fifth day since leaving Los Andes, I cycled into the colonial town of La Serena.

Arriving in La Serena early the next morning, I decided to journey immediately into the valley. Cycling out of La Serena, a city cooled by the Humbolt, warmed by the sun and misted each morning by the combination of the two, I had strayed from my track. That I might ride in a valley seeded in turn by desert and mountain excited me. Feeling tireless climbing out of the saddle, I was soon out of sight of the city. Compared to the grim mania of the Pan-Americana, this valley would be one of generous abandon.

On either side of the road, women were bent double picking flowers from blue fields. The crop was for the *vino grallo* – the wine of the valley. The fruit for the *pisco*, was piled in big whicker baskets which creaked as they were carried. Tractors were spraying vines that soon would produce some of the finest wines in the world. Watering the leaves of plants in the desert is as much to do with hope as survival.

A crowd of cows, watched over by a couple of cowboys astride Wassau ponies, were munching, and from where I stood by my bike, they sounded like echoes in a crisp packet. Along the Elqui river valley, the mist began to unfurl, dissipated by a sun just beginning to shine.

From La Serena, a road leads into the desert, and then to the mountains. The shrine of Gabriela Mistral I knew would be part of those mountains. She was a Nobel Laureate and in this valley drenched in biblical heat had the status of a saint. She described the valley as 'confined yet lofty, many-sided yet simple, rustic yet a mining area'. The road up the valley had been repaved as far as Vicuna, where 'its branches all lead to fertile nooks, to shady vegetation, to dense groves, to gardens fed by the very sap of the hills'. Of the Elquinos, the people of the valley, she says that 'even the most taciturn of them come out with witty and charming remarks'.

In Chile all the main roads lie parallel to the Pacific Ocean. Occasionally one shoots off either to the west, to the beach, or east into the desert or the mountains. Some of the routes go further, finding their way into jungle, swamp, or plains. On the sunrise side of the Andes, Argentina possesses the plains, Bolivia the jungle and on the manky, untrodden side of Peru, whatever is left.

Further into the valley, the hills became loftier and the river began to race. From the road I could see a *parroquia*, a style of church without a permanent priest. Telescoped by tall pine trees, a dusty track led to the plain earth-coloured frontage, which was simple and magnificent. In the flying-doctor tradition of the great outback, priests pass through here only on Sundays.

All along the valley farmers continued to spray their vines with water borrowed from the river. In between the vines, houses were thatched with *totora* – river rushes – and surrounded by trees bearing *chirimoya*, a small pear fruit crossed with a banana. As I climbed towards the east, the air became drier, for the land was no longer cooled by the sea breeze. Such an arid zone supports a hardy way of life. Dogs staggered in the heat, their tongues in the dust; horses lay flat in the shade, panting noses snuffling in the grass. The sound of crickets was getting more voracious, more immediate, a little more desperate.

In the area around Vicuna, capital of the valley, there are mines of manganese and copper, alluvial gold washed down by the river. I rode past orange groves and pear trees and tasted from orchards the most succulent apples. Bags of dried fruit sold from roadside stalls vied with handwoven rugs from the wool of sheep from nearby Chapilca. Dusty tracks led off to Paihuano and Pisco Elqui where table wine sat in casks, waiting for another day of festival. And perched on a peak overlooking this valley, the Cerro Tololo Inter-American Observatory houses the largest reflecting telescope in the southern hemisphere. The purity of the air and the clarity of the night sky makes this district of La Serena one of the astronomical centres of the world. The square plaza was heavily shaded by trees with big leaves, and between the shade of the bars and the plaza, there was a gentle stream of people.

On 6 April 1889, Lucila Godoy Alcayaga was born in this little Chilean town. Of Spanish, Basque and Indian descent, she grew up in the mountains and became a schoolteacher at fifteen. Her reputation as a poet was established in 1914 when she wrote *Sonnets of Death* in three parts. Signing them with a name coined from two of her favourite poets, Gabriele D'Annunzio and Frédéric Mistral, Gabriela Mistral became the first woman in South America to win the Nobel Prize for Literature. It was the time when Latin American literature turned away from modernism. Vicuna could only be simple and direct.

Less than an afternoon's ride from Vicuna, in the village of Monte Grande, lies the grave of Gabriela Mistral. A small track, like a pencil-line in the sand, led me towards this hidden village on the lower slopes of the mountains.

I was looking down on the world from ledges, cliff-hanging

85

on the broad shoulders of an ever more steep valley side. Patches of green rice sprouts poked out of paddies glistening like mercury on both banks of the river. Tiny tractors wriggled over fields, turning ground in the never-ending cycle.

All afternoon I cycled. All afternoon the sand of the road turned more and more to dust. Tired and pummelled, I arrived at Monte Grande, a minute settlement shaped by a church and a row of eating houses around a parched village triangle. The reclining atmosphere I knew well. The plaza looked like a trade route where hippies, backpackers and the occasional cyclist met at sunset. I was home. Yet I was so blistered and hot. Sore from the sun and the grinding of the bike against a hard road. Pushing the machine across the plaza to a line of white-fronted parlours, I joined a group of boys sitting by their packs.

'You come far?' One said to me as I lifted the bike to lean against a post. 'La Serena.' There was a shout from inside the building as a boy and girl raced to see the bike.

'Color! Color!' and they pointed to the frame. They were in awe of its colours which sometimes take on the quality of plumage.

'I have this maximum and minimum philosophy,' one said to me, eyeing my front low-loaders. 'Here I have nothing but my pack and I am happy with life.' Pausing, he smiled. 'You must know this, you carry so little. But in Santiago, I have everything, and I do not even like to get out of bed.' I smiled and asked a woman at the hatch for a cold drink.

'Tell me,' the other one said. 'Why do you come on a bicycle?'

'Because it's all I know. I've always travelled on my bike and it's cheaper than buses,' I said, smiling.

'But it is not too hard?'

I shook my head. 'Sometimes, but not so much if you're a cyclist, and anyone can be one of those.'

'So what do you see on a bicycle that you don't see on a bus?'

'I see the same things as you,' I said, 'but just occasionally there is more to seeing. I mean, have you ever been so crazy that you howl like a jackal chasing *nandus* along a road that is a thousand miles long?'

'Must be good stuff man . . .'

'What is . . .'

'What you see on that bicycle,' he interrupted, 'to go crazy like that?'

Pulling my lips wide I made a grin like a jackal. There was a pause. And then, 'So what do you think of Chilean people?'

'I like them.'

The boy laughed. 'Every stranger feels they have to say that, no, what do you *really* think of us?'

'Catholic and provocative,' I replied.

'That's because you can't get into the girls like you do back home,' he said snorting.

'Everybody shows off in the plazas . . .'

'Yes. They are the parade grounds of *La Familia*. You are right, they show off.'

'I think people flirt a lot, you know, and maybe such expressions are warmer here than where I come from.'

'What is flirt?' he asked inquisitively.

My Spanish and his English couldn't help here so I winked at him and watched his maleness precipitate into a crisis.

'Yes, that is the way it looks,' the other boy said quickly, 'but you know there is a reason for that. We are in fragile times and more than ever before, the people of Chile must stick together. The family is our unity, stronger than a thousand years of corrupt rule.' I just sat down with my drink and listened. Their talk was sometimes prickly, but on and on until the sun went down and the cold goose-pimpled our skin, they talked.

The boys, smoking to keep warm, unified by the road, were working out the relative abstract qualities of each other, to see if they had changed by being in a different place. They told me about a magician who lived in a cave further up the valley who made oranges appear from nowhere. And so warm was the atmosphere, under the auspices of mountains so gold, I didn't have the need to disbelieve such a story.

Steering in the sand had become a problem, so I had to repack a few items from my panniers; both sides had to balance. I had travelled so far with so little. A bus pulled up by the triangular plaza from which more *mochileros* retrieved their back packs from the boot. In Spanish, a *mochilero* is a cockroach. In Chile, you were either a tourist, a cockroach or a hippie.

A few yards out of town on the promontory of a small hill, the bust of Gabriela sat proudly, guarding the town as a schoolteacher would look over her children.

'Where are you going to sleep?' one of the boys shouted as I led my bike off into the night.

'By the shrine.'

'But you haven't got a tent?'

'No.'

'What about the scorpions?' I was already becoming too far for him to hear me. It was true, I didn't know that they existed here, so it was reasonable to assume that these hypersensitive little earwig bashers wouldn't know about me, so I need not get in their way.

As the light from the moon obscured a starry sky I stretched out to drift into sleep. Gabriela's father abandoned the family when she was only three, so she was tutored by her mother and stepsister. In 1922 she was asked by the Mexican minister of education, Jose Vasconcelos, to assist in his reform programme, and a year later was awarded the Chilean title of 'Teacher of the Nation'. But hers was a life freckled with sorrow. Her first love committed suicide and to her great anguish her second love married someone else.

Her *Sonnets of Death* reflected her grief and 'Dolor' detailed the aftermath of her doomed affair. The winning of the Nobel Prize in 1945 didn't assuage the loss of her nephew, adopted and raised as her son, for he too took his life. She developed diabetes and moved to Long Island, New York where she died of cancer on 10 January 1957.

How often she must have stood here, looking down the valley, watching the dust settle on the square. How often she would have looked out of her residence in New York only to close her eyes to see what I saw now.

SIXTEEN

The following morning I woke with the sun in my eyes. The steps that I had climbed in the night had taken me as high as the rooftops, and from here I could look down on the village. On a higher ledge the stone face of Gabriela had been awake all night, watching the sunlight on the plaza, on the boys of last night who were congregating for breakfast.

Breakfast consisted simply of toast and a boiled egg, but, having eaten little the prevous night, I was ravenous. As I ate, a police land-cruiser patrolled the edge of the plaza. '*Rosco, rosco,*' muttered one of the backpackers snorting, before resuming his meal. It was strangely predictable to see young middle-class travellers react in this way to authority when soon they would be offered just such positions.

'Are you going to see the magician?'

'Reckon so. If it's as hot up the valley as I think it's going to be I'll probably need a magic orange.' I said this trying to crack a joke, but these boys, foreheads creased, took their magicians seriously.

'When you get up there,' one of the boys said quietly, 'to El Colorado, look to your right, into the base of the valley and slowly scan the hillside until you see a cave. That is his summer residence. Ask for Charlie and if he's not there, try by the river, he lives there in winter.'

I thanked him, paid my bill and left.

It was less than twenty miles to El Colorado up a little known pass. I twisted along a valley floor, along a path, strewn with rocks that served as lookout posts for lizards. My progress slowed to stumbling speed. All morning I humped the bike into and out of rock pools fed by tributaries of melted snow. All afternoon I climbed through verdant woods which echoed with birdsong and a distant stuttering of cicadas that seemed to staple the heat to the ground. Lazing on the track, snakes, thick and powerful with green and black stripes, seemed contemptuous of my passing. And as the morning drifted into midday, and in the spiced blur of Chile, I saw houses scattered on the skyline.

Cracked lumps of plaster surrounded the base of each house. Red clay-pipe roofs were chipped away with age. So still was the air I felt myself smoulder rather than sweat, but the climb thankfully was over. Sipping water from my bottle, I sat for a moment on the edge of the road and scanned the hillside for Signor Charlie. At first I saw only the barren slope of a mountain mighty against the sky. Then I saw the bushes, speckling sunburnt spaces between the rocks, and then dark shadows. Finally, high up the mountain on the far side of the valley I spotted a cave.

I had the eyes of a mole rather than an eagle, but on the edge of this hollow something was hanging. Leaving my bike next to the house, I walked down a steep-sided slope, separated from the opposite bank by a stream determined to reach the sea. Crossing over a bridge with loose planks, I waded through bushes of gorse, sandwiched between boulders; before, the size of stones, and now as tall as turrets.

Ahead of me, and much lower than the cave, I heard snoring. Walking to a hut strung together with cardboard and polythene bags, I saw a small bald-headed man sleeping like a baby. It was siesta time so I loitered by the edge of the shack, heartened to hear a magician snore. As everything else in the valley seemed asleep, I too began to nap.

'So you, boy, what you do here, spying on me?' Someone was trying to nudge me awake. 'You want drink, here, take this.'

'Are you Charlie?' I said, rubbing my eyes. 'Charlie the magician?'

'Ah, magician, yes . . .' And without saying any more, he handed me a glass of gritty red wine which tasted as if it had been heated on a shovel.

'The boys at Monte Grande told me about your orange trick, and . . .'

'No, no oranges. It is a simple thing. When they come here, these boys have already magic in their head. You know, some people see what they want to believe.' Charlie wore a crumpled blue shirt and baggy trousers tied around a portly waist by string. Littered about were empty bottles of Sangria, their screwtops having been chucked into nearby bushes. 'So . . .

you have come to see me?' I had, and I didn't know why. 'You want me do tricks, like monkey?'

'Your friends seemed impressed.'

'Impressionable friends,' he said sardonically.

'Why are you here?' I asked.

'To confound stupid question? Who are you? . . . Ah, what does it matter, you probably don't know.' For a moment he was impatient, but repented. 'OK, sorry. I have still sleep in my head.'

Inviting me into his home we sat on the floor, three bottles of *pisco* alone and dead in the corner. 'Life,' he said. 'Life bring me here, and here I stay until it take me way. That what you want hear, the hippie crap? Man, I here because I have no money and no work. Better alone in desert than city.'

'Why here?'

'Oh, lots of travellers like you. I do deals, you know. I survive,' and he laughed. 'To tell you truth, I live in Santiago all my life with wife and cheeldren in house with car and job selling . . . oh I forget.' Pulling out a fresh bottle of wine from under a box he slowly unscrewed the top. 'What you write?'

I had pulled out my diary and was recording a little of what he had to say.

'Ah, memory's images, once they are words they are finished, like a photograph, you carry in pocket and forget in head.' Scratching around the floor he blindly found a cup and glass and poured himself and me a drink. 'You know why I no write? Because I talk my story and in ten minutes my story is spent.' The wine was sweet, the bottom of the bottle appeared too quickly.

'Come on, let's walk. I take you to meet people you like. You heard of "fire people"? . . . No, well I take you, better you stay there than here.'

Before I could answer, he stood up and led me by the arm and walked me down towards the river. 'They very crazy people these people, they talk of space people and I think they have much money to talk like this. You know, people like you come, work for them for nothing, can you imagine work for nothing?' Shaking his head we crossed the river when he briefly spoke to a man, who was loafing at the water's edge, and who eyed me furtively.

'Come, we walk this way,' and leading me up the side of the mountain he paused only to buy grapes from a man carrying a sackful. 'Carry these,' he said giving them to me. He didn't

speak until we reached the road, where my bike lay as I had
left it. Charlie stood over it and looked at me. 'Where, my God
has this come?'

'It's mine.'

'You have come far.'

'Far enough.'

'Come.' He walked off along the dusty track and picking up
the bike I chased after him. I didn't know where we were
going, but the afternoon sun was warm, the effect of the wine
strong. 'Years I live here, years away from city, and when
there, I think everything possible, all part of big dream. You
know I was that dream. My mother she say, "Charlie, you be
careful not go too close to people, you might catch their
dream." City is same. City dream same. Now I know with
every want there is things you cannot have. You know, like
desire, a fear.' He paused and pointed to a valley that, when
unbearably hot, merely becomes less so. 'What you think I
have here that Santiago has not?'

'Nothing?'

'Nothing and everything,' he said, putting his arm around
me. 'Here you cannot have dreams of city that has desire and
fear and many rules that I not understand. Here you have only
what you see, no rules. Against mountain with so nothing to
grow, here is nothing to hide . . . come this way.'

He pulled me towards a path leading through scattered vines
while I dragged the bike, keeping poor time behind him.

'You know, I think that the priestmen got it wrong. I read in
city much crippled, and old, and in India you hear of cheeldren
make noise because no food. I think myself who made these
people. They not like in shape of God, or God too is monster.'

A chill ran through my body, a chill that against such a sun
could mean only danger. For a moment I felt vulnerable. I was
like vermin for an eagle and should the man at the riverside
think me easy prey it would be unfortunate to have travelled
so far, to be seduced on to a mountainside deep in the heart
of Chile, and then be pulled apart for the little that I had.

'Charlie,' I said instinctively, 'am I safe?'

He didn't answer immediately, being a little out of breath,
and I noticed he had developed a limp. Taking the grapes from
me, he put his hands on his knees and wheezed. This gave
me time to assess the situation, look around through the piles
of hanging fruit for any sign of a predator.

'You are tired?'

'The bicycle has become heavy,' I said. 'How far is it?'

'Fifty metres. Around the next big bush.' I saw no one. Heard no one tracing our path. Yet the air was so still it reeked of suspense and tingled with electricity like before a storm. Looking down the hillside, Charlie peered towards the road, scanning our climb. He seemed surprised to see only a valley and a field full of vines. Then he bent down and picked up the grapes. For a full five minutes we stood, breathing more and more quietly until the sound of footsteps pierced through my senses and made my heart savage my chest.

'Ah, Charlie, *buenos días,*' from behind that bush a little old lady greeted him as if he were an old friend, '*como estas?*'

'*Bueno, bueno.*' And now did I fear to be mugged by her? To kick me with her flat shoes, to wrestle with spindly arms. Charlie smiled, first at her, and then at me. Pausing for a second more, she nodded and continued her way down the hill.

'Climbing to this place I suffer,' said Charlie, 'but I tell you one thing, the last thing I have to say. In this heat it is like fire. You do one or two things. Accept the fire and live on mountain, so much a part that fire is less. Or you work out what is fire, what to recognise, what is fire and what is not, and in all of this, what is not fire you do not put water but give air, and give space to burn . . . come, last walk.'

Slowly we tramped in the dust. In the near distance a row of small buildings designated the end of this journey with Charlie which I knew I could never forget. At the entrance we were greeted by a lady with grey hair and a kind face. Charlie gave her the grapes, saying nothing. He stood there, uncomfortable, saying goodbye to me before turning away. I watched him walk out of sight.

On the 29th parallel and high in the Andes, the air is clear, perhaps the least polluted on the planet. It is here that this lady, Sister Christina and her followers, listen to the sound of the cosmos. More UFOs have been sighted over El Colorado than any other place in the world. Here, each individual is addressed either as brother or sister, sharing duties marked up on a blackboard. Sister Christina explained a philosophy that in Spanish I could not understand. But it was time; time for the celebration. A small group of followers ambled into a building designated the temple.

'Come,' one of them said, 'but take off your shoes.' My heart sank. I knew then I was potentially the unwilling precursor of a disaster. I had the feet of a potentate; they were stinking richly, like the sun-dried intestines of something squashed. As I sat cross-legged in a circle of people facing Sister Christina, the balm of my feet crawled up my body like a fart. This made it difficult to empty my mind of all things earthly.

Each day the group celebrated the rising and setting of the sun, its exact departure, from or to, a horizon hidden by the mountains, calculated with a watch and a set of tables. In the centre of the group, Sister Christina sat before a small altar, piling it with cow-dung and ghee as she repeated a quiet, melodious mantra. Checking her watch, she lit the ghee, and ringing a small bell to signify the onset of meditation, the altar burned, the sun had set and my feet began to embarrass the rest of my body. I noticed through my nearly closed eyes someone from across the room looking at me. If all the sewers of Calcutta could be distilled into a pair of socks, that look suggested it was I who was the genius that had procured them. When the sun had set and the bell had been rung, I put on my shoes and left.

28

29

30   *Puno, sitting a little untidily on the shores of Lake Titicaca.*

31   *Tourist snaps of Uru Indians at Lake Titicaca: a culture being asphixiated by greedy commercialism.*

32

33

34   *Driving his donkeys each day past the magnificent ruins of Ollaytaytambo – made magnificent by archaeologists – was a nuisance for this man; most days, I suspected, tourists would get in the way of his donkey.*

35   *Machu-Picchu railway station. The colour of this scene was so vivid it didn't seem real. Reality back home is often less exciting and takes on a shade of grey.*

36   *Ingapirca, Inca fortress in Ecuador.*

37   *Views across Patagonia.*

38

_____SEVENTEEN_____

It was three cycling days to Copiapo. When I arrived in the main plaza I hunted down the same hotel in which I'd stayed during my first visit to Chile. The Hotel Carrera was down a side street of the centre of town. Its small rooms surrounded a courtyard. The patron's wife greeted me at the door and the old patron, apart from being a year older, appeared much the same. From this little courtyard a year ago, my solo expedition to the summit of South America's highest mountain had begun.

Deteriorating conditions around Aconcagua had forced me to look elsewhere, and after two days' ride from Copiapo I would be able to see Ojos del Salado from the _alto-plano_. The old man brought me some tea and asked me if it really was I who had attempted the mountain. It was the gossip of the square. I had ridden and climbed to within seven hundred feet of the summit, when the journey ended disastrously at 22,000ft.

The patron was curious. He said many people had enquired about the cyclist going to Ojos.

'Did you find the lodge?' he said. I nodded. He himself had directed me into the desert and told me about a _refugio_ high on the _alto-plano_ where I could rest and eat. After half a day's cycling along a paved road, the route, he said, would become a track and that would climb to the western slopes of the Andes. It would level out at 15,000ft. I had done as he said and for two days I had climbed a severely twisting path dotted with isolated homesteads struggling to farm goats on arid scrub. After riding around a sharp bend, I saw mountains drop to valleys as deep as an ocean trough where the bottom was carpeted with flowers blood-red and gold. The first night I gathered together sticks of wood, and used clumps of _meseta_ scrub for the fuse. I absorbed the heat of the fire which in a true desert is the most wonderful warmth to have.

95

'Tea?' the patron said waking me from my reverie. He was staying up late that night and when I said yes, made his way to the kitchen. And so I climbed higher and then higher, breathing faster and more deeply, the air beginning to thin.

On the *alto-plano* the sun shone through a sky which was innocent and blue yet possessed a cold bite that could kill. Peaked crests of mountains were blindingly white with snow. For hours I rode over slabs of metamorphosed rock, powdered from mountain form. I was riding to the old man's lodge. Hour after hour I expected to see the mountain. *Ojos* translated as 'eyes' and *Salado* as 'salty'; Old Salty Eyes would be waiting. A convoy of vehicles caught me with an arsenal of flying stones. They said the lodge was nearby.

'More tea?' Placing the cup by my side the patron settled down to read the paper. 'If only I had tea on the mountain,' I thought. Anything to keep me warm. It was so cold, so very cold I could hardly breathe. But it was too late. I was finished, some would say before the journey began.

The lodge was built to commemorate Louis Murrey, a geologist working for the Anglo-American Mineral Corporation. Bob, my host in Santiago, was the Exploration Director for South America. When Murrey and his pilot crashed their helicopter on the summit of Ojos, Bob, refusing to let the memory fade, had the lodge built as a memorial.

It was very comfortable and the food was good. Bob invited me to dine with the team of geologists and asked me if I was serious in my quest, to cycle to the summit. That I was there was answer enough.

'You must treat the mountain with two things,' he then said gravely. 'You must give Ojos compassion, and integrity.' He paused. 'Wait a day, acclimatise and then go.'

I said I would wait. This I did not do.

Sleeping badly through the night I felt strangely good the following day. The forecast was fair with conditions set to deteriorate later in the week. It was now, only now. I convinced myself that waiting would stall the ascent into bad weather. More than that, I was simply unable to wait. With three days' supply of chocolate cake, some eggs, dried fruit and two pints of water, I followed a track.

So intensely did I scour the buffalo-arched summit of Ojos, its shape would forever be imprinted in me. Yet I never looked back and that was my undoing. So determined to go on I forgot to heed what I already knew. The altitude was asphyxiating my capacity to reason and I was unaware of the danger. And for this I grovelled. Losing the track I missed the two higher *refugios* which were both stocked with blankets and food. On my first day up the mountain, I camped wild at 19,000ft.

Gutted with crevices, the route I had taken nearly broke my spirit. But I was so close. The next day was harder. The wind was becoming a gale. Near the summit it began to snow. I could see the top. Less than half a mile . . . I could reach out and touch it. I was in the shadow of the highest peak in the Americas, and it was, for a moment, mine. I made camp, leaving everything except my bike and cameras.

'Sprint to the top,' I thought. 'Get down quick.'

It was a good plan. Setting off into a wind that became increasingly bitter, I began to falter. Twice the wind blew me to the ground where I fell heavily.

'Go tomorrow, put the bike down.' Something in my head told me to stop, but I had never before known how to stop. I tried again, and so forceful was the storm that could last a day or a week, it forced me to walk back into the wind.

By a small crevice I hid my cameras from the flying earth and pressing forward for what seemed only a moment, leaned the bike against a boulder. 'Back to the tent, try again tomorrow.' But where was the tent? 'Back to the bike . . .' but where was that boulder? Here and there, then everywhere, scattered like a dropped mountain were hundreds of boulders which had not been there before. The cameras . . . couldn't find them, panic . . . to hell with the cameras and I began to run but where . . . back to the beginning . . . but which beginning?

I stood and panted in the snow and, with the most dreadful of awareness, I knew I was lost.

From when the sun was at its highest until it touched the horizon I scrambled around the lower summit. I searched with an easy-going madness for a tent that contained a life-saving sleeping bag. That I should find it was irrelevant. The important act was to rationalise the situation and this was impossible. The landscape was besieged by nature at its most hysterical. I was compounding a bad decision with blunders and, after maybe five hours' searching, I sat behind a rock like a foetus and wondered what it would be like to die.

Warm and cosy, I began to drift off to sleep. Blinking in the snow I had never felt so happy. I had every excuse for failure and yet it shook me. So what of fickle success now? What of the path I'd taken to that state of enough and contentment, and what of the boulders in the way? And what about the folks back home? So I began to think through my life but quickly decided that witnessing scrambled bits of the past was less exciting than what was happening now. Here I recognised for the first time something which I always knew, that there is an exact point where you are your past, and frighteningly it was close. There was a slipping away.

Deep within me, some vestigial link with life persuaded that, however glorious and restful death might be, to live one's allotted time was necessary, even if only to exorcise the face of such vanity. Eventually I stood up and looked down the mountain. If only I had looked back on the way here. Should I spend the night in such conditions I knew it would be my last. Picking my way away from the summit I slowly began to descend.

The old patron, having fallen asleep wrapped in his paper, woke with a start, thrashing at the pages. 'Ah, you are still here dreaming?' he said. 'I think too I was dreaming of your mountain . . . so you are here and not there as memory, eh?' he laughed. 'That is good. Now tell me as I was thinking, how long did it take you to get down?'

'Two days,' I said, and he nodded, satisfied with information that certainly tallied with his knowledge of the mountain. I remember cracking holes in streams to drink. I wandered in a moonlit dream of circles. I tried to piece together the route to safety. Each night I allowed the cold to shiver my body into convulsions. The warmth generated from the shaking of my back gave me some comfort. Near the bottom I fell down sand dunes hundreds of feet high when in the distance I could hear voices. They grew louder and more distinct until I recognised workmen hammering into wood.

Faster I walked to the crest of the last dune, after which I heard no more voices and sat quiet on the shore of a green lake. A track led off to my left.

'Do you know,' I said to the patron, 'when I walked back from Laguna Verde, I had to rest for ten minutes for every fifty paces. When I lay down on the track, my back was in such pain I thought it would break.' He shook his head sorrowfully.

'Well you are here,' he said at last, 'and it is late. Tomorrow I will make you breakfast before you journey north. And God speed you.' Rising from his chair he smiled and wished me goodnight.

Four days from Copiapo I crossed the Pan American bypass near Calama. In the distance I could see the Andes, resonant in the shimmering air. From a distance I too would have had my edges distorted. It was midday and the sun burnt into my body whenever the slight breeze became quiet. I pedalled towards San Pedro de Atacama.

The desert appeared flatter the further I rode away from the road. It cut into the ground from Chiloe to here. Much was obscured. Between me and the majestic mountains, deep cuttings and valleys, scar tissue and the droppings of earth-movers had channelled my way north. The Pan American Highway is often unutterably tedious.

Only by enslaving myself to a schedule was I able to continue. It was important to break the boredom. Timed stops which allowed for simple rewards. A cup of tea was my lot, the price a conversation in itself. I liked my tea, it was compensation for the times when single-mindedness was like a drone in the service of his queen, shifting along her debris.

But there was a reason even for this sand-blasted section of the journey. I was here to gather material for a book. But the miles were beginning to wear me down. A twinge in the leg and another muscle fibre explodes, rupturing through to the surface to make the skin turn diesel-blue. Then my hands would peel once again. Not for the first time, that would be too easy. And for as many weeks as the journey will last, my hands will turn red. Then they will burn into open wounds that suppurate on to my handlebars. They go septic, get better, harden and heal and then go red once again and my bum is sore. Standing on the pedals to raise myself off the saddle, the blood rushes through to my bloodless buttocks. Buttocks so sore they would have rendered helpless the Horsemen of the Apocalypse – and with his great steed Bucephalus, did not Alexander sometimes dismount and walk away bow-legged?

Cutting into the interior of a desert that heated up as each mile passed, I began to feel as dusty as the land, no longer crisp and twinky. If I turned the colour of the road I would be camouflaged.

99

Transport stopped rarely. The desert offers no welcome. During the day the desert is not quiet. The wind makes it difficult to listen to the silence which I knew must be there, and the sound of the chain racheting around the back-wheel cogs stopped me from listening to the wind.

Twenty miles passed and my closeness to the foot of the mountains beckoned me on. The sun had reached its zenith and fell on my back. Scrub became rare, and apart from the solitary tree, there was nothing but endless sand. After long, tiresome slopes I sailed the downside as effortlessly as I could. So as not to feel the fatigue I tried not to think of anything and ended up thinking about my bike. It was, I decided, serving two purposes. As a vehicle to carry me across lands complex and strange, it has no rival. That linked strips of metal can fit around plates of teeth to act as the thrust and the drive is genius. To propel moving wheels that allow me to balance is magic indeed. That the vehicle can be steered in any direction with ease is freedom of an absolute kind. But the other use of a bicycle is simpler still.

Three hours after leaving Calama I had endured the heat and the road as much as was comfortable, but from then I knew it would hurt. My water bottles were hot and the road steepened. And up the side of the mountain I slowly toiled. Standing or resting away from the bike was less cool than riding into the breeze, which, like drinking warm water, is better than no water at all. And yet it was I who was creating the thrust on those links of metal that connected with the cogs. It was I who, through a hundred million adjustments of mind and body, made the balance complete. I could claim control for my actions.

And however miniscule my decisions, whether I should stop or go, the laws of motion would mean nothing without them. But more than this, as I reached what had to be the final crest before descending to San Pedro, I steered. And although the track was narrow, a hairline in a desert, it was a different hairline to any on which I had travelled before.

EIGHTEEN

Señor Lopez was a very cheery man. He was the owner of a corner street restaurant and said he was the father to all travellers. He did a good job – his food was hot and cheap. Later I booked into a guest house which had a small room with a window that looked on to a courtyard. The owner slept in a shed with his chickens and rented out his other rooms to travellers. Before travellers started coming here, he said, the chickens had a room to themselves.

San Pedro was an oasis, lushly shaded in the plaza. Old men stood talking, flapping their walking sticks while the ladies sat knitting on stone benches.

That night a group of travellers were being looked after by Señor Lopez. They didn't look very dirty and would not have been able to walk far with the luggage they were carrying. They were friendly and invited me to their table where I shared a meal. They were going to walk into the desert and said I could come along.

It was agreed to walk for an hour. The moon was full so there would be plenty of light. Martin, a blond spiky-haired punk, sitting next to me, began to tell me what he expected from the walk.

We assembled at the police station where Juan Carlos had to attend to some business. Negotiations did not seem to go well. His papers were not in order, but for a walk in the desert we didn't need police permission. When the clock overlooking the plaza struck midnight, we at last stepped out of the building, playing follow-my-leader through the back streets of town.

Under the lamplight of a full moon we were soon stumbling over rocky ground on a patch of desert that surrounded the town, but in reality we were trespassing through the very centre of the Atacama. The party were in search of the remains of the most southerly Inca settlement, Tulor.

Martin was jangling along about halfway down the group,

the fast pace of Juan having straddled us over several hundred yards. Tall, with a sneering laugh, Martin carried a miner's lamp around his waist which clattered against a thick metal-studded belt. Juan Carlos executed his actions with a loud voice, his baggy knee-length shorts quivering as he talked. The trek would take at most a couple of hours, but no-one had a watch so timing had to be under the jurisdiction of Juan or the moon.

Behind us, low-roofed houses that reflected the sun so well in daytime, transmitted an eerie glow from the rising moon. The moonlight was absorbed by the grey igneous litter of the rock-strewn landscape. Still, there was enough to see where we walked and so I coasted up to Martin and offered him an orange.

The trees lining the periphery of the town had receded and, to our right, looking like agar on a culture plate, rocks on the horizon began to grow into mountains. The desert plains were beginning to open out to us and like cattle escaping into a field of wheat, we were invited to gorge in the beauty.

'Oh what wonder,' Martin gasped, 'what wonder!'

I thought it was flat and ugly.

'I am energised by the desert,' Juan exclaimed to the group. 'The site of Tulor is less than an hour away,' and, wide-eyed, he strode purposefully on.

'Didn't he say that an hour ago?' I said to Martin.

'Could be. I'll ask Enrique.'

'Er sure, whatever you say, man,' said Enrique who had begun to giggle inanely whenever anyone spoke to him.

'Big mushrooms, eh?' said Martin as Enrique began pointing at the moon.

Thanks to Enrique, the moon continued to gravitate towards a distant horizon against which two trees were silhouetted. I wanted a rest.

The roots of the trees would have stretched far to support such naked twigs in this waterless land. 'Martin,' I said suddenly. 'I'm going back. I can do without all this effort. I spend every day along the edge of this place and I'm off again tomorrow.'

Martin nodded. 'This man Juan is walking far and we are not equipped. Already we have walked three hours and I do not see the site, but I want to continue.'

Enrique walked close by, talking alone, his words pinking like hiccups.

'Tell the others I'm staying here for a while before returning,' I said and taking an orange I had saved for the journey, I offered half to Martin and his girlfriend while the other half would serve as my inducement to be alone.

I watched the group slowly filter away in the distance. Stretching in the sand, I wondered how many people must have leant against such a tree. And before that, what then, perhaps next to the tree where man was born. According to the Nuer such a tree stood to the west part of south Sudan, where the root of life was cast and thrust up. The descendants of early man would also have had such a tree, poking so bravely from out of the ground. In my travels I'd collected an old Dinka song which an old tribesman had once sung to me:

> *In the time when Dendid created all things,*
> *He created the sun,*
> *And the sun is born and dies, and comes again.*
> *He created the moon,*
> *And the moon is born, and dies, and comes again;*
> *He created the stars,*
> *And the stars are born, and die, and come again;*
> *He created man,*
> *And man is born, and dies, and does not come again.*

So to this tree the Inca empire began to push south. Early in the fifteenth century, in the reign of the eighth emperor Viracocha, the Golden Empire began to expand. The emperor's son Pachacuti completed the conquest of the Titicaca basin but it was his grandson Topa who pushed into the Atacama itself.

For the Incas, the desert represented conquest of territory, salt, minerals and gold, and a place of worship. But for others, the desert means so many things. In 1788 John Ledyard killed himself in Cairo in brutal anticipation of a journey into the Sahara. Two years later, Major Daniel Houghton, a fifty-year-old bankrupt wanting only to flee his creditors, met his death at the hands of Moors. Mungo Park found himself a lonely captive, perishing of thirst, amidst the wilds of Africa.

And here I was, a speck of dust on the same sea of destiny. Different tensions had to be understood and dismantled. Nineteenth-century travellers ventured wherever they wished.

Then, marauding brigands chased latterday explorers for game. Now the danger is losing your passport. I've met guards who extort money from travellers. With their dollars they get drunk and rape.

'The faculties of the man who goes into battle,' said W. H. Hudson, 'are inflamed with instinctive expectations that are sharpened to a joyous preternatural keenness.'

But compared to Mungo Park, the Incas or those much maligned travellers, I am constitutionally timid. Only after experiencing my own such moments in the achievement of total solitude, can I look back with a strange glory that can never be forgotten.

The desert wind was flicking through my hair, its cool fingers playing a lullaby around my face. In the darkness, in the desert, I have often thought of more perfunctory matters. What must it be like to make love in the desert? I closed my eyes and old thoughts began to remind me of a woman I saw in Uganda who was dressed like a tiger. Her hair was black like the mane of a stallion, her body animal-like with sweat. Tiger-dotted and the colour of skin, her dress clung to her body, and as she stood in front of me, acacia bushes dappling her with shadows, it was as if she were naked.

It took several attempts to find the right route back to town. I eventually found the dried bed of a river and so followed it downstream. It wasn't the direction I remembered, but in a desert you can journey in circles. As the moon set, an oblique glow cracked open on the horizon, and as a glint of the sun appeared, I stumbled into town and into bed.

Around midday I woke and breakfasted at the restaurant. Señor Lopez said he had just seen Martin and Danielle stagger into the police station but there was no news of the others.

'But they had no food or water,' I said.

The old chap paused. 'Ah yes, it is not the first time that this has happened. The police will be informed and one way or another they will be found.'

The following day I cycled away from San Pedro, back along the same road on which I had ridden a week before. I have never liked retracing routes. On a bike, movement is forward only, and then unilinear on a track. Precious effort appears to count for nothing when you can see your own tyre tracks before you. Perhaps there should be greater expression on a bike which is too constrained by that narrow hairline road. It's easy to say from an armchair that freedom of movement equates with freedom of expression. I have cycled in sand and know how much it hurts.

But there was another reason for not wanting to return along a route I had already cycled. When I started cycling around the world I was always getting lost. Boarding on the wrong ferry, back alleys in Endhoven. Time after time I tucked myself into a dark corner waiting for morning to kill the confusion of night. Later I began to ride in the dark. It was a gutter in Bangkok or the streets of Los Angeles; turgid, stained night with the rattle of violence that was always in your head. And then I got lost up a mountain and nearly died.

As I lay down near the summit of Ojos, I was happy, too happy to want to live. Then I began to think that defecting from a route in Chile is no worse than getting lost in LA. If I fell delirious at this very spot, 1,056 miles from Santiago on a fractured little road in the Atacama, and walked off into the desert, I would almost certainly die. If I cycled through the centre of LA during a normal workday lunchtime, I could ask a policeman to help me on my way.

But it could be different. If, for some reason, I did or said something here that the authorities didn't like, I have some reason to believe that a policeman may put his hands on my shoulder and take me away. In Los Angeles, some punk from out of the shadows could do it for less; and there wouldn't be anyone, let alone a policeman, who could help me then.

NINETEEN

It was such a lovely ride across the desert. The snow peak of the 18,000ft Licancabur Volcano glistening in the sun. After about ten miles on the road I remembered Señor Lopez telling me to watch out for the Valley of the Moon. Here, fantastic landscapes are caused through the erosion of salt mountains and hidden ores and nitrates become iridescent at sunset.

The road heaved and buckled and I climbed two long rises in the morning, only to freewheel with a beautifully warm tailwind for most of the afternoon.

Life was good and I felt very happy. What I like about being happy, is that it's as if you've never been sad. Scavenging in my pannier I pulled out a banana. It was firm and, without stopping or slowing down, I skinned it with the famous one-hand banana trick, and ate it. As a child I watched David Carradine in *Kung Fu*, and wanted the young monk to snatch the pebble before the master could clench his fist. When he was doing that, I was cycling around the lanes of Cheshire squeezing banana all over my handlebars. It could take a lifetime before I might learn how to make it pop out intact. But if only a guru could see me now; flick-side-peel and a tighter grip from the palm. So my Herculean task is to cycle around the world until that one day when I get it right.

There is a story about two young Buddhist monks who set out to search for a great sage from whom they could learn. Gently they travelled far and wide in many lands before they found the one they sought. When they found him he was already old and tired, and surrounded by many other disciples who had also needed him. He welcomed the two friends and asked each one why he had travelled so far in search of a teacher.

The one said, 'I have come to listen to you and learn from

40   The train to Machu-
Picchu at Ollaytaytambo: like a
sickly looking orange caterpillar
with camera lenses for legs.

41   The arrival, it is said, is fundamentally an anti-climax after the approach. Machu-
Picchu, with the higher peaked Huayna Picchu, disproves that point: the approach so hard,
but the arrival sublime.

42   *Canari Indians on the road to Ingapirca. How they grab at me, pinching my arms and laughing. Yet if I did the same to them, they'd form a ring, crush me to death with their bosoms and the men would stand around and laugh.*

43

you. I will be your disciple and want you to teach me all you know.'

The sage smiled and said, 'In that case you may stay, and I will teach you all I know. And you,' he said, turning to the other monk, 'Why are you here?'

'I came to be with you.'

The sage appeared not to hear him at first, then standing to leave he said, 'Yes, you too may stay.'

The two young monks shared a cell, and together they attended all the discourses of the great sage, gathering with the other disciples. The one engaged the sage in learned discussion of the scriptures, and the sage taught him all that was in the commentaries and the arts of debate and of reason. The other not once took any active part in the discussions. To him the sage said nothing.

After some years the old sage called the two to the sacred tree where he always held his discourses. He told them that he had given his last discourse and would devote the remaining years of his life to the pursuit of Nirvana. Both were dismayed and asked what they should do. To the one he said, 'You came to learn, and I have taught you all I know. Go back to the world and teach others to be learned; none is as well versed in the art of reason as yourself.'

To the other he said, 'you came to be with me. You have become me. Stay and help others to be wise.'

The Atacama desert was not as difficult to cross by road. The building of it would have been a greater adventure than mine.

It was four days' ride to Arica and there I stayed with friends of Juan. They were kind, generous and likeable hosts. After a day writing postcards, I decided to leave my bike in Chile and continue to Peru with local people. Thoroughly bored with my own company I wanted to go to Machu Picchu on a bus.

Tacna was 25 miles from the Chilean frontier and 40 miles from the port of Arica. Under Chilean control from 1880, it was voted by the people back to Peruvian jurisdiction in 1929. In an unsuccessful attempt to Chileanise the city, so many schools were built that Tacna has the highest literacy rate in Peru, the best hospital, the cleanest water, and an airport suitable for jet planes.

Tacna also has a cathedral. Designed by Eiffel, the construction began before the Eiffel Tower and was completed in the 1950s. But around the city the desert was tawny.

I was directed to Salida Tarrata, a market area on the edge of the desert, where, I'd been told, there were buses journeying to Puno. Once there, I was directed back to town, a red Chevy taxi taking me to a door, behind which I heard someone typing. Not here, I was again told, tickets could only be purchased at the market, so I doubled across the city. No, the market traders said, I should go to Avenue Bolognesi behind the cathedral. No, not there either.

So I went to the market and sat in a café, where ketchup stains had dribbled down the wall like blood. Normally I would have cycled 85 miles, but today I'd crossed Tacna city three times. Bus stations all over the world seem to suffer the misfortune of careless people nervously on the move. This one was seedier than most. Rain had not fallen for years and municipal workers existed only to lean against tatty street shacks, squirting wads of coca screw on to anyone who didn't see it coming.

I waited until evening for a bus to arrive and when it did I was allotted a place on the floor. Squeezed between two Indian women who moved with the grace of dumper trucks mating, I fell into their lap as the bus heaved forward.

It would take all night to reach Puno, which on the shore of Lake Titicaca was 12,000ft high on the Peruvian *alto-plano*. Here you fight to get on a bus, but with a smile. As the bus began its route, climbing high to the crest of desert, the edge of Tacna had turned into habitable rubble.

Soon we jerked and stumbled over the Andes. The roughly hewn road narrowed, hanging over precipices that slipped down to distant valleys. We rocked for hour after hour. And so the long summer's day became the abyss of night. It was impossible to sleep and, although I was tired, the bus was distinctly easier than the bike. There was a scream. Next to me a commotion was brewing. The local population were Indians who spoke Quechua, also known as *runa simi* – which means the language of the people. It was a trade language spread along the coast at around the time of Christ. I understood only the occasional Spanish word and whatever was translated to me.

'The driver, he is drunk,' someone explained. The bus had been veering dangerously, but that seemed normal. Now it shot forward in a series of spanking movements. The lights inside the bus were switched on then off, and, as we began to plummet, the headlights illuminating a nasty switchback, several woman began to wail.

The men from the back tried to calm the situation and the driver said it was only light refreshment.

'Eight beers at lunchtime,' I heard someone say, 'was not light.'

The brakes screeched, throwing everyone forward into a communal skid. Without warning, something soft and mountainous had placed me into complete darkness. The bus had jammed to a halt. Gasping for air, I realised that one of the Indian woman had landed on me, her warm sweaty bosom pinning me to the floor.

Someone shouted 'The *gringo*! the *gringo*!' and slowly I made out in the darkness a crowd of concerned passengers laughing as they winched the woman back to upright. I returned slumped into a seat, dazed with my lovemaking in Peru.

The driver was equally abashed. He looked like a rat who had climbed out of a bucket of white spirit and was incapable of bolting from his corner.

'I know the road, you know,' he said, 'and I am not alone . . . God is my co-pilot.' The bus shuddered with laughter. 'But he is not driving us. You are,' someone else shouted, and at that, the driver slumped over his driving wheel. Opening the doors, an army of woman crammed on to the side of the road. With *montera* bowler hats tipped, gathering their wool skirts, they began to laugh at their own plight and mightily they pissed.

And when it was thought the driver could stand, passengers once more allowed him to drive. Smiling like a pig who had avoided the chopper, he threw the gear-stick forward and once again the bus lurched its way towards Puno.

Puno was an austere town where slabs of houses without gardens opened on to cold streets swept by a bitter wind. Edging along the highest lake in the world, past red-cheeked peasants leading scraggy llamas by string to market, the bus pulled into town. Breakfast cafés were opening and, after ordering milky coffee, marmalade baps, orange juice and apple pie, I breathed deeply in the crisp mountain air. Without my bike I was a more obvious species of tourist and, try as I might,

I would never be allowed to relinquish my grip on the modern world as I stepped into these dark ages.

In Peru there are 5,000 Indian communities but few densely populated settlements. Nearly 99 per cent of the rural population and 60 per cent of town dwellers have no running water and their diet is 40 per cent below acceptable levels. Their literacy rate is the lowest of any comparable group in South America, but this was of no consequence to their most recent ancestors. The Incas, in the manner of medieval troubadours, employed a caste of professional historians to hand down the public record in the verbal tradition. It hadn't really changed.

After breakfast I walked to the edge of town, where, moored to a small jetty, launches ferried locals to islands poking out of the choppy waters of Lake Titicaca. Along a road squirming with wretched dogs, men with black suitcases stepped from doorways and tried to sell me tickets to visit the floating villages of the Uru Indians. Trucks steamed in pools of diesel, metallic colours separating into a steel rainbow. And in the rain that began to teem, the road dissolved into mud. Little kids' noses streamed as they squatted on the pavement.

Although I've seen it a hundred times on such manky corridors of poverty, it doesn't make it any easier to own up to the truth. For the first time on my journey I was not able to cycle away from the shit and the squalor. Here I had to walk slowly past people who deserved more than this, a gentleman voyeur who surely could make do with less.

TWENTY

Full of bowler-hatted women and men sporting trilbys, the launch waited for me to board before setting off to Amantani. It was a two-hour ride through the Golfo de Chuchuito, past a jutting peninsula that protected the Urus from a lake with the characteristics of a sea. The reed islands bobbed, making smoke from straw shacks waver as the whole village undulated. Sheltered in the half-covered deck, the women tended babies, while the older children swopped well-chewed gum. The young girls were round-faced and pretty, their eyes darkened with black-liner, the tops of their ears toasted brown by the sun.

On deck, two travellers swopped tales, basking in a sun that had sneaked away from storm clouds which pinned down the mountains. He was bald and Australian, looking forty but said he was twenty-nine.

'I live frugally,' he said. 'My parents provide me with free food and rent and I save and travel. What I piss against the wall is my only loss.'

Eventually the launch reached the island of Amantani and, after stopping briefly in three inlets we anchored in the fourth. The two *gringos* and myself jumped from the boat on to a small harbour wall.

'Here,' the German said, opening negotiations for the rent of a room, 'I have him down to a dollar.' Fifteen minutes later he had reduced the nightly rent by ten English pennies.

'Still too much,' said the Aussie. 'This boy says eighty cents.'

I left the other travellers and walked along a rocky path up the side of the island to a plaza. There, framed on a terrace by a small hall glazed the colour of white sugar, the air clacked with the sound of a typewriter. Sheltered from the breeze, the static air incubated a heat that made thinking hard.

Nothing moved here except my eyes, prising from the stillness a clue. I needed somewhere to sleep. In the corner and

111

set in shadow, a small restaurant displayed a sign advertising a room for hire. The patron, a wiry little man, led me through to a back courtyard full of squeaking pigs where we climbed a ladder to the converted loft of an adjacent barn. The room was painted strawberry pink, the bed covered in a patchwork quilt, and a mouse's window looked out over Lake Titicaca. So enchanting was this room that the air sung with a butterfly resonance. And spilling out of a brown-paper packet on to the bedside table, what looked like privet were in fact *hojas de coca* – leaves of coca. The patron introduced himself as Miguel and asked me if I wanted some coca to chew.

The coca shrub grows at altitudes ranging from 3,000ft to 8,000ft on the subtropical eastern Andean slopes known as *yungas*. The Incas cultivated the shrub on coca fields called *cocales*. Containing alkaloids of which cocaine is the most potent, these leaves serve as a central nervous stimulant, a local anaesthetic and an appetite-depressant. An Indian who chews an ounce of leaves a day consumes about one-fourteenth of a grain of cocaine, which is a very tiny amount. In Peru, the consumption of coca leaves is legal and useful at altitude.

'*Lejia*,' he said, 'made from burning of *quinoa*,' and he passed me a stick of grey lime. 'Eat with *hojas*.' Wrapping several leaves around a fragment of lime, he placed the coca ball into his mouth and sat as entranced as a hamster. Only the juice was to be swallowed and having copied him, I did likewise. I could hear water sloshing in the yard. A rooster's call near the window and the cries of children filtered into my room with precision. Slowly my mouth began to numb and if there was a rush of well-being it was slight, but my senses were acute.

There are many legends associated with the origin of coca. One Peruvian legend from the sixteenth century tells of a beautiful woman killed by the Indians for her sexual indiscretions, and from her body grew the coca plant. Across the lake in Bolivia, legend there says that the god of snow and storms became angered by the smoke created when the Indians burned the forested eastern slopes of the mountains for farming.

Sending a storm that flooded the *yungas* and destroyed the roads, the people became isolated. When they came out of caves used for sanctuary, the Indians found their lands devastated – the myth of the Deluge on the *alto-plano*. Someone discovered a mysterious shrub and after eating its leaves, all who tried felt happy and strong, their hunger pacified. Bringing the plant to the highlands they gave it to the wise men (*amautas*) and healers (*yatiris*).

Contemporary Bolivian Quechua legend speaks of coca as the daughter of Pacha Mama (Mother Earth), born as a sacred plant with the power to vanish evil. So protective is this power that coca leaves are burned whenever someone moves into a new house. An offering of twelve perfect leaves, a little red wool and some llama fat are placed on a fire. The smoke of Mama Coca penetrates the house, drives away the evil spirits and then ascends to the sky in the ghostly form of a human body.

Miguel was quiet and I was thoughtful, influenced as much by the scene from the window as the leaves. Coca grew on terraces that led down to the lake, beyond which was the distant shores of Bolivia. Eating coca here was like drinking coffee. Historically, coca was a divine plant to the Incas, often used as an offering in religious rites. Only Inca nobility were allowed to chew the leaf and this right was one of the most prized gifts an Inca could confer, burying them with their dead nobles so they may be sustained in the afterlife. More practically, the Spanish distributed coca to the Indians when they discovered how much harder and longer they could work for less food when allowed to chew the leaves. As an oblique form of currency, coca was worth a fortune. In the nineteenth century a Corsican named Angelo Mariani introduced a red wine made from leaves he called Vin Mariani, à la Coca du Perou.

Pope Leo XIII was among those who enjoyed his daily tipple. But the breathrough came in 1885 when an American called John Styth Pemberton introduced French Wine Coca to the people of the United States and so created one of the most teeth-rotting, gut-stomping and stomach-bending imperalist phenomena in the world . . . Coca-Cola.

Much as I should have liked to dream a while in my pink room, I had to cycle along the coast of Peru to Ecuador. The next morning I jumped on the boat motoring back to Puno and that afternoon set off on a night bus to Cuzco, arriving under the auspices of a watery sun trying to shine on the centre of the Inca universe.

It would be remarkable even in Spain [wrote one of the conquistadors, Pedro Sancho about Cuzco]. It is full of palaces and no poor people live here . . . Most of the buildings are of stone, or else faced with stone, but there are also many adobe houses, very well built, arranged in straight streets crossing each other at right angles. All the streets are paved, and each has running water in a stone-lined gutter down the middle. Their only fault is to be too narrow: only one mounted man can ride on either side of the channel.

But according to Inca legend, the founder of the empire was Manco Capac, a child of the sun, who had been set down with his sister on an island in Lake Titicaca. There, he had been given a rod made of gold and was told to grow the seed of the empire wherever the rod should be wrestled to the ground. Journeying to the broad and fertile valley of Cuzco, he lost his grip on the rod and there the foundations for the city were dug. In 1440 the city was replanned by the ninth Inca, Pachacuti Inca Yupanqui, whose noble architects employed 20,000 men.

Shaped in the body lines of a puma, the central area of the city was overlooked by its head in the guise of the great stone fortress of Sacsahuaman. In the south there was the tail and the body was the plaza, the Huacapata – the Holy Place – where the Empire's most important ceremonies were performed.

There, each day before sunrise, a fire was lit and food thrown into it for the Sun's sustenance and appeasement. So noble was the last of the line of Emperors, Atahualpa, so young and haughty, he commanded a palace guarded by 2,000 soldiers, while beside the inner door there stood a hundred captains well experienced in battle. Interestingly, at whatever cost to genetic harmony, Incas married their own sisters who bore their men offspring. On top of this, the nobles also maintained a large harem. The royal harem lived in a convent near the Temple of the Sun and numbered nearly 700. Selected for their beauty from the most aristocratic of Inca families they were themselves attended to by virgins.

They had the privileges of the garden of precious metals but, should she transgress her vow of chastity, the virgin would be buried alive, and her accomplice hanged, together with his wife, children and servants.

114

Brought to the royal palace they acted as ladies-in-waiting, serving the needs of the royal Inca. So when the day's business was done, the Inca would be served by his concubines, feeding him with their own fingers from a gold plate placed before him. If he hawked, a woman would hold out her hand to catch his spit; if a hair fell from his head, a woman would pick it up and eat it, so preventing it from falling into the hands of an enemy who might bewitch him.

Yet so aware were the noble Incas of beauty that in the very gardens of precious metals, according to the conquistador historian Garcilaso,

> there were planted the finest trees and most beautiful flowers and sweet smelling herbs, while quantities of others were reproduced in gold and silver . . . There were also all kinds of gold and silver animals in these gardens, rabbits, mice, lizards, snakes, butterflies, foxes and wild cats. There were birds set in the trees and others bent over the flowers, breathing in their nectar. There were golden deer, pumas and jaguars and all animals in creation, each placed just where it should be.

Most of the finest examples of Inca walls are situated around four small quarters of the city, centred around the intersection of San Agustin and Maruri and Cabracanche. I walked down Calle Plateros to Calle Saphi, where there was a small hotel that had been recommended, along the most magnificent walls. The Incas' skill as masons is their most wondrous artistic legacy.

They succeeded in cutting and polishing their stones with a simple virtuosity. Adjoining blocks fit together with no recognisable mortar; joints appearing as scratches, bevelled for the purpose of artistry and interlocking in polygonal patterns, each block or *ashlar* withstanding earthquakes when all about had fallen down.

Once black and made of andesite, here the walls had weathered to a reddish-brown. Others were made of a greenish-grey material from Sacsahuaman hill and a hard, grey stone from the Yucay limestone. The Inca walls were so stunningly beautiful. And by these walls stood my hotel.

Less of a hotel, more a bed and breakfast, it was called Familiar.

There I would stay for a day before moving on to the ruins of Ollantaytambo and finally Machu Picchu. I stepped into a small, tiled courtyard overhung by a balcony and ordered a coffee.

Suddenly I heard someone say, 'If you can't put ketchup on it, it's not worth eating.'

Sitting at a table next to where I stood, two fellows, obviously English, were chatting over breakfast. Pulling up a chair I asked if I could join them.

'I had all the symptoms of typhoid,' said the one with a large bushy beard and straightaway began to describe the details. 'I sweated a lot, threw up a lot and shat a lot.'

'That's shitting in the vernacular,' his mate said in a strong scouse accent, 'only past tense 'cos he's posh . . . yea, and keep away from me yer 'airy Brit.'

'Andy the beard' was from Nottingham and the fellow from Liverpool was called Dave, both on their Peruvian holiday.

'You know what a greasy café job is?' Andy said to me as Dave shov̇elled down a whole egg, his eyes helping its ingestion. 'You know, fag ash Lil doing a rasher of bacon and a very dead egg and you asked for a breakfast . . . well, I got an Inca one last week.'

'Inca-redible,' said Dave.

'You need a supplement of nuclear-charged anti-diarrhoea pills round here –'

'Or stick sumert' big in yer gob to stop yerself eatin' yer daft sod,' said Dave and ordered more coffee.

A girl came in and sat down next to Dave. 'I've just been to the station and entered into another huge South American cock-up,' she said with a voice from the Bronx. 'I waited two hours in the wrong queue to buy a ticket for an Indian train that no longer exists, but my book says it does.'

'I reckon we get the tourist train for nineteen dollars, give the message boy a few intis and he does the queueing,' said Andy sipping his tea, 'and then back to the Cross Keys for a game of arrows . . . Machu Picchu's alright but I could down a pint of ale,' and he raised his hand to his mouth holding his imaginary glass.

'All yer've got to do is pick-up these little Peruvians and move 'em to one side,' Dave smiled at me. 'After all we've got Ibrox and Heysel behind us, nothin's gonna stop me gettin' a ticket.' He got up to leave. 'If yer fancy a chat in the room later,' he said to me, 'pop in.'

After an hour of idle talk, Andy and I got up and joined Dave where they said I could sleep in the third bed that was spare.

'Play the game, know the rules and you'll be OK,' he said. 'And if they get too close I've always got this.' Strapped to his calf under his trousers he pulled out a long razor-sharp knife.

Dave was a hard breed of traveller who somehow expected the worst from his journeys; maybe he was right. He bought coke in Lima, got busted in Panama and was ripped off for a hundred dollars on the way to Cuzco; exciting in its own macabre way. He described how after being womanless in Saudi, his efforts exploded a 'johnnie' in Río, and I was filled with a rush of nostalgia for the solitude that I could afford on my bike.

TWENTY-ONE

It was not going to be too difficult to reach Machu Picchu. The following morning I walked to Calle Huasca and jumped on a bus to Urubamba, two hours' ride into the Sacred Valley of the Incas. There I walked through a market, bought a meal of fried trout and paid a few intis for a ride on the back of an open-topped Datsun pick-up to Ollantaytambo. Down a road leading away from a sad-looking plaza, I saw the most amazing flight of Inca stone terraces that exist anywhere in their former kingdom. Cut out of the cliff-face each terrace was at shoulder height, and at the head of this most sacred valley they occupied a crucial place in Peruvian geography.

Surrounded by trees that dripped in a perpetual mist, the terraces formed the junction between the Andes and the Amazon basin. The air was now studded with swarms of biting borrachudo flies, and coral snakes shited in the forests. Below, the river Yucay-Urubamba roared over rapids that had at last sunk into the beginnings of low jungle. I climbed to the top and looked down the valley which was sheathed on all sides by cloud. What Manco Inca's warriors must have seen when successfully defending the terraces from Hernando Pizarro in 1536 would be as I saw now.

After a night's uneasy sleep in a room near the base of the terraces, I got up early and walked along a track by a stream to the station to wait for the train; there was no road to Machu Picchu. There were two trains due to arrive and the first one would not be for me. Lingering in steeply forested slopes, fingers of mist licked the trees wth the debris of discharged storm clouds. Indian women sat on the track, their baskets of eggs and cooked meats ready to be raised.

I sat for an hour waiting for the train to come and then it did; snaking round a corner, its orange and cream carriages wrapped around fingertight windows. Everyone jumped to selling position. This was the tourist train. On its arrival people photographed Indians without asking, home movies their only concern. Woman raised their baskets to the doors, trying to sell a few morsels to blotchy faces, behind telescopic lenses, which recoiled at the prospect.

When the second train stomped in noisily an hour or so later, the baskets were ravaged by a hundred arms poking out of the carriages like the legs of a centipede. Wth pockets stuffed with meat and eggs I jumped on board.

At Machu Picchu station all tourists were herded on to buses that shunted back and forth up a switchback road that delivered its passengers to the entrance of the ruins. The entrance was carefully guarded and access through the turnstile was allowed on production of five dollars.

The city that emerged was simply a place of wondrous beauty. Set amidst tidy terraces the houses and temples were intact to roof level. The sugarloaf of Huayna Picchu stood like unshaven jebels in the Nubia, like the horn of a rhinoceros gift-wrapped in wisps of mist that hung over a steep-sided canyon hundreds of feet below. And there, following each other in the way elephants join trunks to tail, hundreds of tourists circulated in the rain.

Sheltering under a lintel spanning the entrance to a house lower down on the slope, I just sat and gazed.

Sifting among the debris of my pocket I retrieved, scribbled on a piece of paper, the 'The Heights of Machu Picchu' by Chilean poet Pablo Neruda. It had been saved for the occasion:

> *Then*
> *up the ladder I climbed*
> *through the barbed jungle's thickets*
> *until I reached you Machu Picchu.*
>
> *Tall city of stepped stone,*
> *home at long last of whatever earth*
> *had never hidden in her sleeping clothes.*
> *In you two lineages that had run parallel*
> *met where the cradle both of man and light*
> *rocked in a wind of thorns.*
>
> *Mother of stone and sperm of condors.*
>
> *High reef of the human dawn.*
>
> *Spade buried in primordial sand.*

119

This was the habitation, this is the site:
here the fat grains of maize grew high
to fall again like red hail.
The fleece of the vicuna was carded here
to clothe men's loves in gold, their tombs and mothers,
the king, the prayers, the warriors.

Up here men's feet found rest at night
near eagles' talons in the high
meat-stuffed eyries. And in the dawn
with thunder steps they trod the thinning mists,
touching the earth and stones that they might recognise
that touch come night come death.

I gaze at clothes and hands,
traces of water in the booming cistern,
a wall burnished by the touch of a face
that witnessed with my eyes the earth's carpet of tapers,
oiled with my hands the vanished wood:
for everything, apparel, skin, pots, words,
wine, loaves, has disappeared
fallen to earth.

And the air came in with lemon blossom fingers
to touch those sleeping faces:
a thousand years of air, months, weeks of air,
blue wind and iron cordilleras —
these came with gentle footstep hurricanes
cleansing the lonely precinct of stone.

Hiram Bingham was brave, enthusiastic, curious, a mountaineer, and an historian. He was also very lucky. His account of his discovery of Machu Picchu is majestic.

'In the variety of its charms and the power of its spell, I know of no place in the world which can compare with it.' Hiram Bingham had found the Urubamba Valley.

Not only has it great snow peaks looming above the clouds more than two miles overhead and gigantic precipices of many-coloured granite rising sheer for thousands of feet above the foaming, glistening, roaring rapids, it has also, in striking contrast, orchids and treeferns, the delectable beauty of luxurious vegetation, and the mysterious witchery of the jungle. One is drawn irresistibly onward by ever-recurring surprises through a deep, winding gorge, turning and twisting past overhanging cliffs of incredible height.

Here and there under swaying vines or perched on the top of some beetling crag, Bingham tried to understand the bewildering romance of ancient builders of a bygone race, but 'space forbids any attempt to describe in detail the constantly changing panorama, the rank tropical foilage, the countless terraces, the towering cliffs, the glaciers peeping out between the clouds'.

Passing an ill-kept hut they aroused the suspicion of Melchor Arteaga, the leaseholder of these lands. However, the prefect of Curzo, J. J. Nunez, had sent on an armed gendarme, Sergeant Carrasco, to smooth the way. Arteaga said that there were some interesting ruins further on, on the top of the opposite mountain called Huayna Picchu and on a ridge called Machu Picchu. Bingham's companions instead wanted to chase butterflies so he decided to go alone with his half-curious minders.

The next day it drizzled and Arteaga had to be paid a Peruvian silver dollar before he could be coaxed out of his hut. And stepping over a recently killed snake, in the land of the viper on 24 July 1911, they journeyed. The lance-headed viper was a very ferocious serpent. They were later to learn that it was capable of making considerable springs when in pursuit of its prey.

Across a bridge of slender logs lashed with vines they crossed a raging river. Hands and toes across the bridge, they crawled to the other side. For one hour and twenty minutes they had a hard climb when shortly after noon they met two Indian farmers. Richarte and Alverez were like eagles in a nest and there they had lived for four years. They were generous hosts and gave the party water and cooked sweet potatoes. Nine thousand feet above sea level wiith only a precipitous track to the top gave them enough space between them and officials looking for army volunteers or collecting a tax. Instead they burned clear the land around the lower terraces and planted crops of sweet and white potatoes, maize, sugar cane, peppers, beans, tree tomatoes and gooseberries.

All around, tremendous green precipices fell away to the rapids of the Urubamba and immediately in front, on the north side of the valley, was a granite cliff rising 2,000ft to touch the clouds. The heat was great and the humidity high. Hardly had they left the hut when Bingham and the sergeant were confronted by a great flight of beautifully constructed stone-faced terraces, perhaps a hundred of them, each hundreds of feet long and ten feet high. The ancient Inca soil was still capable of growing maize and beans.

Yet this had all been seen in the Urubamba valley. They had not yet found what they sought. He knew he was close. He smelt the rank, fetid bouquet of tension, rot and genesis. Where was the principal city of Manco and his sons, the Vilcabamba and University of Idolatry?

As they rounded another small promontory Bingham walked towards one of the finest examples of masonry he had ever seen. Matched ashlars of pure white granite, diminishing in size towards the top of the wall, produced lines flowing with grace and delicacy. It was fantasy. For Bingham it must have seemed like an unbelievable dream.

Dimly, I began to realize that this wall and its adjoining semicircular temple over the cave were as fine as the finest stonework in the world. It fairly took my breath away. What could this place be? Leased to a man who lived in a hut and farmed by two laid back Indians, Machu Picchu was about to be opened to the world. Surprise followed surprise in bewildering succession.

We came to a great stairway of large granite blocks. Then we walked along a clearing where the Indians had planted a small vegetable garden. Suddenly we found ourselves standing in front of the ruins of two of the finest and most interesting structures in ancient America. Made of beautiful white granite, the walls contained blocks of Cyclopean size, higher than a man. The sight held me spellbound.

Would anyone believe what he had found unbelievable? In a world of diminishing returns who would recognise almost pure fantasy? That the outpost of the Inca Empire, touched by the rain and the clouds and the sun and the thunder, had hardly, in the last three hundred years, been touched by man.

But as Bingham said, 'Fortunately, in this land where accuracy in reporting what one has seen is not a prevailing characteristic of travellers, I had a good camera and the sun was shining.'

_____TWENTY-TWO_____

After two sleepless nights hammering down the Andes in a bus to the coastal plains, I returned to Arica and retrieved my bike. Immediately turning north I crossed for the last time the Chilean frontier, made my way to Tacna and without stopping began the 800-mile-long haul to Lima. So little of this section of the Pan-American Highway was to be exciting – a journey sometimes promises so much, and so often gives so little.

As I cycled out this Peruvian summer morning, the adventure was becoming a battle between me and the barren route. On this road, grey as ashes, hot as the devil, the violence of the heat bruised the crumbly ground. The road looked like a scar on which I rode grizzly and hard from Tacna through Moquegue. Past llama-shaped hedges and roofs thatched with sugar cane and clay, past fields of parched earth buckling like copper, I pedalled in and out of narrow valleys, winding past vineyards that sagged with air thick with dust, as prickly as pepper.

Racing on the bike each day from the rising of the sun until the moment it disappeared, I held on to the handlebars until the webbed crevices of my fingers cracked and rubbed raw. Hour after hour I spun the wheels, sometimes thinking, sometimes not. Bewitched and bored in equal measure I suffered the cycling with all the arrogant finesse that a poor man on a bicycle is obliged to possess.

Three days after crossing the Moquegue river, the road veered and climbed inland towards Nazca, a small colonial town of 25,000 people set in a green valley, marginally above the mist that blew in from the sea.

The one person I had hoped very much to visit in Nazca was Maria Reiche, a German mathematician and expert on the strange and phenomenal Nazca lines. After spending over thirty years standing on stepladders to study lines etched into

123

the desert, she had recently died. Maria Reiche was inspired by Paul Kosok, a former native New Yorker and one-time conductor of the Brooklyn Civic Orchestra. Kosok brought the lines to world attention and 'cleaned' them by shuffling along their path in heavy boots while dragging a stone behind him.

Why the *pampa* should be covered by lines like a scratch pad is one of the archaeological mysteries of the magnitude of Stonehenge. Like tracks in a railway shunting yard, lines approximately sixty yards wide stretch across plains north of Nazca, and occasionally across the Pan American Highway. Sometimes straight and parallel, at other times they run to a geometrical pattern that at first appears to defy all reason.

During her thirty-year study, Reiche also discovered the etched shapes of a bird expressing her wings, a monkey fleeing, cartwheel spokes converging on a hub, rectangles, triangles and a double spiral. Because of the restrictive policies of the Spanish Crown, such discoveries were left unrecorded until the late eighteenth century. I saw just one line intersect the road, the shape of which was meaningless at bicycle height.

Completing her seventeenth year of exploration looking down at the lines from her ladders, Reiche concluded that they led directly to the rising and setting points of celestial bodies on the horizon. Outlining her theory, she said that 'the ancients believed there was some mysterious significance in the way one star would set below one horizon and another star would appear in the opposite direction'. Kosok described more of what I saw from the road as 'the largest astronomy book in the world'.

Reiche found at one place on the *pampa* a small centre containing four solstice lines, two equinox lines and one line for the midpoint between solstice and equinox, the 'eighth of the year'. Such a position it was reckoned indicated a point in time near 6 May, harvest time in the Andes. Astronomer priests could determine the times of the year for planting crop, and relate that to the annual appearance of water in the rivers by using the lines to predict the positions of celestial objects.

Reiche spent her life sleeping and living in the open, existing on a diet of fruit and nuts. Often she would walk into the wilderness following a track for weeks before returning to her field base at Ingenio near Nazca. To me this one line across the road was little more than the drag of a truck, but to Reiche it represented something to do with 'precession'.

Simply, this meant that when looking at the stars, there

appeared a surface of the heavens that contained such bodies in a fixed position. Precession – the movement of constellations – was about one degree per century and occurred as the rotation of the earth's axis shifted. A period of precession – when the stars regain their old position, having gone full circle – is 26,000 years. Reiche said that fifty years was enough to notice such positional changes, something the ancient astronomers would easily have observed. Whenever these bodies no longer rose or set exactly on their allotted line, a new line would be etched.

Nazca was of little interest to me other than that her lines were positioned close by. I doubted ever to return again, and made to stay longer, looking along the line to the distant horizon where the mountains cut of the plain. Lines are believed to have been etched on this, the Pampa Colorado sands by three different groups; the Paracas people 900–200 BC, Nazcas 200 BC–AD 600 and the settlers from Ayacucho around AD 630.

My favourite theory suggests the Nazcas flew in hot-air balloons, and this is supported by the discovery of burn pits used to launch the craft, where, at altitude, the lines can be best seen. Pieces of ancient local tapestry and pottery depict balloonists and legends of flying men, which some say relate to the lines as landing sites for UFOs.

Georg A. Von Breunig (1980) discounts the above, claiming the lines are tracks for running contests. He bases his argument on the asymmetrical surface level at curves in the designs, and in the triangular field which he says agrees with human running characteristics, where a number of runners start off from a straight line and spread out naturally.

And by observing comets in the sky and understanding earthly auguries taken from animals offered up in sacrifice, the Inca Viracocha is credited as being the first of the Incas to foresee the coming of the conquistadors. The Indians say that after events had proved the exactness of his first dream, the elders and high priests of the Cuzco temple began to question him on the subject of his night thoughts. It was on one of these occasions that Inca Viracocha warned of a bearded man who would crush the Empire and the religion of the Incas. So that the people might think their rulers less than eternal and godlike, it was secretly decreed that nothing of this dream be transmitted except from ruler to ruler.

So on I cycled, the momentum of the journey in full swing, the pedal arms thrashing, the spokes of the wheels dicing the passing wind. Once again the bike had performed its functions faultlessly; minor mechanical discrepancies must in honesty be laid at the door of the perpetrator of motion who struggled each day to stay upright on his machine.

Stopping by a roadside café, I wheeled the bike in sight of the bar and ordered a beer. A drunk came up to me and stood an inch away from my face, '*Amigo* – cigarette?'

I shook my head and he spat on the floor, phlegm seeping through his lips.

The old lady behind the bar returned with a bottle from the fridge. '*Sí señor. Felicidades.*' The drunk walked off.

'I am half-crazy from the desert,' I said to her.

'*Ah, sí,*' she said shaking her head. 'Beer?'

I nodded. Reaching out for the glass I caught sight of her eyes, flickering like bedlam. The glass she gave but the beer she snatched away.

'Hundred and forty intis,' she snapped. 'Now pay before you do not pay.'

'But it's usually only a hundred and twenty,' I said.

'Gone up.' She leered her thin lips.

'When?'

'When you came in,' she cackled.

I didn't argue. It was 7.00pm and still that evening I had another twenty-five miles to ride. A youngster touched the bike and it crashed to the ground. The drunk returned. I sat under a poster of Linda Lusardi displaying her boobs, and I looked at her voluptuousness. What would this half-mad old woman think of her here? How did she get to be on a café wall on the northern edge of the Atacama Desert in Peru, when I had sweated across every heat-shimmering metre guided by eyes no longer able to focus? My aching, spindly body was desperate in comparison.

'They don't care about me.' The old lady made me jump from my thoughts. 'I am seventy-two, tired, and they work me to death.' She, like me, was made mad by this desert.

'The desert is hard,' I said.

'It never stops, Señor,' she said simply. 'It never stops.'

The further north I cycled the more barren the coastal strip became. Between Nazca and Ica, small irrigated areas were ever on the edge of thirst. From Ica to Lima there grew only cacti and scrub. Three days after journeyng from Nazca I rode into the capital city of Peru. There I had sanctuary with Martha and Graham, people I'd met in Punta Arenas.

During my stay in Lima I wrote nothing in my diary. The journey was closing down. Terminating at the next country, Equador was last on my list. Taped on to my handlebars were the following instructions: 'Tierra del Fuego, Patagonia, Chile, Peru, Equador' – *in that order* . . . really, how predictable. So for the rest of the week I steam-rollered towards Tumbes, a frontier town on the border of Peru and Equador.

Cycling along the road I saw a man beating a dog. It was yelping and would have run away except that it was tied to a post with a rope. Asking the man to stop I knew would appeal to the part of his nature that was deeply ashamed by his actions. To my amazement he complied and let the dog go. I knew the dog would return, but at least it had the afternoon to lick clean its wounds.

There is also a story about a man who once ruled these lands with immense cruelty. So vicious was his need to rule the Inca Empire that Atahualpa reigned wth blood. The male population was so cruelly stricken that fifteen women existed to escort each man and not a family nor village escaped his vengeance.

Garcilaso de la Vega, a great Inca writer who recorded the events, said it was the day after his death, the dead man being a nephew by a first cousin of de la Vega's mother, no less a man than Atahualpa's son, Don Francisco. The few Incas still alive gathered around the house where the burial was to take place. An old Inca walked slowly to the mother and, smiling, said this was a time for a feast. He offered her his congratulations instead of his sympathy. He hoped that the great Pachacamac would grant her long life in order that she might have the satisfaction of witnessing the death of all her enemies.

'Inca,' said de la Vega, 'how can you ask such a thing when we have lost someone so near to us?'

The old Inca became wild with rage and in the way an Indian would show fervent anger, he grabbed the lapel of his mantle.

127

'How dare you,' he burst, 'it was he, Atahualpa who destroyed our Empire. It was he who killed our brothers, spilled our blood. He committed every crime that is sacred to our ancestors. Allow me time with that man and I will eat him raw. He is but a bastard and a son of a bastard! Atahualpa's mother must have sinned with a Quito slave to give the world such a monster. I am ashamed that you can think the blood in our veins is any way related to the blood of this man. You do the memory of our ancestors a disgrace and wrong us all.'

The old Inca continued like this for some while. The list of ill-doings was mercilessly long. Remembering the misfortune that Atahualpa had bestowed on his people they turned again to mourning and even the Inca was seen to shed a tear. The hatred attached to this man tarred all who were near.

Don Francisco spent his last days socially despised. Couped in his own house he was unable to venture outside without hearing a shout of traitor. Such unwonted hatred would surely follow him to his grave. Alas, the fate of his sisters would be at least as awesomely sad. As the dog was tied to the post, people are tied to their past.

TWENTY-THREE

After a week's cycling along the coast of the northern territories of Peru I was beginning to feel estranged. The places and people passed by, entering into my mind long enough to be remembered. That was all. But at times the bike was a charger, its pump my lance. And away each day I rode like fury, each mile eaten and spat out on bushes.

Yet at every turn my journey was eclipsed. It was obvious that this had to be so. When Pedro de Candia approached Pizarro and said, 'Sir, I am going to journey in the valley, and if I do not return you wll be but one man less,' he also knew that, should he succeed, Pizarro would have an even greater conquest. So, donning chainmail that came down to his knees and the boldest headdress he could find, he grasped hold of a mighty sword, and a shield of polished steel. In his right hand he held a wooden cross that measured every inch of three feet.

After being commended to God by his companions, he bade them farewell and went ashore. Step by step he walked towards the city of Tumbes. The Indians had spied the ship and were amazed by the man's beard. They knew he was not of their kind, so they reasoned it be better to treat the stranger kindly that he might be a God.

The elders of Tumbes decided to unleash in his path a wild tiger and lion which they kept for their King Huaina Capac. Such beasts should have torn him to pieces but instead they curled at his feet and submitted themselves to his will. Pedro de Candia comprehended the situation, God his Saviour had given him the courage of a giant. Stooping down, he stroked their heads, holding the cross above their bodies. So here was the son of the Sun, thought the Indians, and they treated hm to sumptuous hospitality.

As I pedalled through Tumbes, a scabby dog flew at my feet with the wrath of an open wound. Apocalyptically it says in

Ecclesiastes that 'a living dog is better than a dead lion' (ix, 4), but I felt bound to disagree.

Having arrived in Tumbes I sat by a plaza in a café in the shade. I longed so much to converse without my being hampered by my limited Spanish. Seating herself opposite me, a woman traveller began to stare. Dowdy and greasy, she had a beetle-like face with spectacles more suited to withstand sun-flares than to see through. She offered me a drink of papaya juice. Our conversation quickly developed around her work in Nicaragua, her socialism, her travelling, and her life in Canada.

'Do you know,' she said, 'cyclists think they're so special. The last one I met spent two hours talking about cycling and didn't even ask me my name!'

Picking up her glass she finished her juice and ordered another. 'My name is Ellen,' she said, 'and I'm a born-again Christian and last year I got married. My brother-in-law is a gay florist in Toronto—'

'Oh yes —' I began, but she verbally stoned what I had to say.

'. . . Exciting isn't it, you know, everything . . . so my brother-in-law did the flowers and my mother-in-law, who had disturbance problems, believed her son was being kidnapped by me and goes to get the police. And so the service continues half an hour late without her. She and that goddamn flower-picker arrive with the police and try and stop the service . . . well God, you never saw anything like it. My man was carried out by his mother, his puffy brother was in tears and Woodrow Woolley, our vicar, just stood there the sweet man, with his wife in her pink halter-necked dress . . .'

Glancing instinctively towards the plaza I managed to break from her fixed stare – but the plaza was devoid of people.

'. . . Well we were already married by then until this loony accuses him of being a spy on our honeymoon and that puts him in a depression for ten months and end of marriage.' Slamming down her glass she ripped into laughter.

On the pretext that she had spotted someone across the plaza whom she recognised, Ellen left me abruptly. She struck me as an interesting lady with a complex about cyclists. So I too drifted into the plaza and began looking for a room.

Tomorrow I would be in Equador, where they say the air is sweeter than in Peru.

The sloping road to the border of Peru and Equador was peopled by pot-bellied nylon shirts stuffed with wads of heavily thumbed money. Frontier culture sometimes slips in its own pus, and in this respect Peru was very adept. So I continued my journey north.

Unlike Colombia much further north, and more so than Peru, Equador still has a large ethnic Indian population. The Otavalo Indians of Otavalo in the north were known as the Cara and came from Colombia a thousand years ago. In 1455 the Inca army moved north from Peru and after seventeen years of fighting overcame Equador and eventually the Cara. Near Otovalo is Yaguar Cocha (Bloody Lake), so named after the bodies of slain Cara warriors who were thrown into the waters.

Yet strangely, an historically questionable legend tells of a Cara princess married to the Inca Huayna Capac, the Inca son Atahualpa given from the union. This interestingly connects with the Salasaca Indians of Salasaca near my route north to Ambato, who wear the mourning gown of Atahualpa. Originally living in Bolivia they were transported to Equador as labour colonists for some transgression or rebellion.

The Incas had two categories of *mitimaes*: seriously recalcitrant groups were sent faraway into the heart of the Inca Empire that they might be watched over by loyal Quechua; the second category of *mitimaes* was composed of loyal Quechua used to supervise the peripheral edges of the Empire. The Salasacan community suffered the lesser of the two fates and ever since have remained adamantly closed to outsiders. Called *los bravos* they resisted incursions of roads, missionaries and all forms of foreign culture.

Anyone who marries into the community must adopt Salasaca dress – black poncho or *manta* and a flat, wide-brimmed hat. The connection with the Inca is, according to Salasaca legend, that the black poncho is worn in mourning for the death of Inca Atahualpa, who was killed by Pizarro in 1533.

Within miles of leaving the border area the air became moist and warm. If Peru had made the journey arid on the coast then Equador would make it tropical. I rode past Arenillas and Pasaje and climbed into the mountains to Giron. Settlements called *anejos* or *parcialidades* consisted of thatch-roofed adobe houses separated from neighbours by fields, which, smelling of burnt banana, edged up to their plantations. Since the Equadorian Andes receive much more rain than the Peruvian or Bolivian highlands, Equador is greener and sweeter. In the midst of a banana jungle I thought of my journeys to Sri Lanka, waved up Kandy Mountain by leaves of papaya. I remembered the cool air on the equator at Bukittinggi as here I dripped and dried. After the paradise of Lake Toba in the Sumatran highlands, the road dropped to the torrid swampy heat lower down at Sibolga. It was like that now.

As the road climbed back to the mountains, the heat eased. I wanted to see the stones of Ingapirca. After riding through Cuenca I was in the valley that would lead me there. On the road to Azogues the sun shone with a brittle warmth suggesting it was still summer. Poorer than Cuenca, Azogues sat resignedly amidst peeling whitewash and tinny donkeys. Suddenly the road began to rise and steeply. My legs responded wearily and my arms began to wobble. The rate of deceleration was close to a collapse. This hill had become a monster.

Pressing on the pedals, heaving round the cranks slow and tediously, cycling up that hill was menopausal, so rapid was the change to my metabolic rate. Not a woodpecker nor birdsong could penetrate my thumping head, but, turning from a descent that was draughty with free-spirit, I knew the hill was simply a part of a time that had to be endured. But I heard a lorry. Ah yes, I knew what to do. Humping its way up and wrapped in a band of metallic air it began to ease past. It drew level with me, its wheels higher than my head. As it pulled away, I lunged for a rope hanging from the tailgate and hung on for as long as I could.

At the top of the hill there was a café. Sitting at the only table was a lady built like a frigate in a floral patterned dress. Excusing myself, as the English are wont to do, I sat opposite her.

'I'll have a coffee and some toast,' she said to the serving girl. 'and I'll write a letter to my friend,' she murmured to herself while looking at me. She turned her attention to a blue plastic shopping bag and began to stir around the contents before emptying everything on to the table. The knuckles on her hands had dimples, the mobility of which were restricted by the thickness of her fingers.

'Too much writing, and they are never actually sent. And where is my book?And where is my paper?' Through jagged nostrils she breathed stentoriously. This is not like an elephant, who whistles down a fingery trunk. So this is travelling, I thought, the process of which is often no more than dialogue in a bar.

'I write four letters at once,' she said, 'using carbon paper. . . three sheets placed between four pages.' Frisking around red welts on fat shoulders, she searched for a dress strap that was trying to escape down her arm. Finding it, she heaved it back to position.

And so we write. I in my diary about her, and she in her letter about me.

'Where did you say you were from?' she asked, pausing while I gave her the name of my street. 'Oh,' she said. She hadn't heard of the street, but it was in a town not far from a city in the northern part of a country she once thought she saw on television.

TWENTY-FOUR

Ingapirca is known to be a fortress but as usual there are conflicting archaeological reports. John Hemming says:

> the central structure is an usnu platform probably used as a solar observatory. It is faced in fine Inca masonry, and it is interesting to note that the length is exactly three times the diameter of the semicircular ends. This may have been connected with worship of the sun in its morning, midday and afternoon positions.

Climbing out of the bustling town of Canar, the centre of influence for the Canari Indians, I rode up a steep and broken track past columns of broken Indians.

The Canari had a highly developed culture in the Cuenca Basin, even before the arrival of the Incas. Their copper tools, their textiles, pottery, and their gold jewellery are beautiful. When the Canari attempted to resist the sweeping forces of the Inca Armies, they were killed in their thousands as many of the rest were sent as *mitimaes* to Cuzco. Once the Cuenca Basin was secure, Topa Inca built the palace of Tomebamba near the city of Cuenca. Topa's son, Inca Huayna Capac, was born there. Later he built the fortress of Ingapirca. When Huayna Capac died in Quito in 1527, the Canari naturally sided with his son Huascar during the civil war between him and his half-brother, Atahualpa. Both chaps claimed to be *the* Inca and as the conquistadors postured as cavalry, Huascar fell. For such services, Atahualpa decimated the Canari tribe.

As I cycled past stumbling faces it seemed as if the Canari had not recovered. It was a festival day and everyone was clutching clear bottles of colourless liquid. Fat women staggering with their *shigra* purses and macramé bags, swigged hard from their bottle as they tilted thick necks forward. Behind the women came the men strumming on drums and mandolins.

The only allegiance the Canari tribe paid Atahualpa was

their willingness to become allies of the conquistadors after his death. When in 1533, Pizarro had Atahualpa strangled and burnt, the Canari would have celebrated then as they do now. Handing me a bottle, an old fellow picked at my saddlebags for anything that could be removed. The liquor tasted like the devil and had the power to burn clean old sores. Pulling the men away, a group of women scrummed around, poking with sticks and breathing with sweat and spirit.

Pedalling past village *campesinos* in their braided skirts and red shawls, I crossed the railway at Tambo. On this festival day the men wore black suits and sported shirts with large collars, and sleeves that supported a large margin of cuff. Eventually I reached the solitary restaurant in the village of Ingapirca. I was to be graced with a hot meal, which that night was all I needed before sleep. A hut beside the site was to be my accommodation. After a plate of potatoes and stew I felt better but sleepy.

The young proprietor sat next to me and we watched an old chap being dragged across the square by a heavy *campesina* woman. As the sun began to lose interest in the day the women appeared to gain interest in their men.

'She has need of her man,' the proprietor told me in broken English. 'She will give him mighty flogging when home.'

The old boy was voicing his protests, but dragged by this giant of a woman, his journey made little sense of what he had to say.

So Ingapirca was shaped as Hemming described and, like a lizard warming in the wispy sun, I clambered over the stones. Except for the shrill sound of a puppy squeaking, all was quiet. At midday the sun would shine nearly overhead but further south shadows would lengthen in the winter months of June. As the sun went further and further down, it was natural to fear the flight of the sun to the north, when those left behind might freeze in the dark and starve.

But the priests were very clever. They knew the secret of *intihuatana*, or 'the place to which the sun is tied'. On 21 or 22 June, the winter solstice, the priests tied the shadow of the sun to a stone pillar in one of their temples. When the shadows began to shorten and the sun was once more overhead, the crops began to grow and the priests were venerated for their great power over the Sun, their god.

By the time the Spanish arrived in the central region of Equador, the Incas had been in charge for over fifty years. The Quito Indians, known as Cotopaxis, occupied the towns of Robamba and Latagunga, which acted as administrative centres for the Empire and were effectively linked by roads guarded by *tambos* or fortresses. By 1560 the Spanish had completely destroyed all known Inca stoneworks, replacing physical traces of one occupation with another. I had ridden in the mountains for two days and was on my way to Quito, to the equator. Each day the clouds steamed and rolled and mists muffled the sound of birdsong. Each pedal stroke ensured there was that much less to ride.

The Incas believed in a creator god they called Viracocha but their primary god was father Sun, Inti Taita. Yet, with a nice feeling for the divine, they worshipped just about anything; Mother Earth (Pacha Mama), Mother Moon (Mama Quilla), Mother Sea (Mama Cocha), Father Thunder and Lighting (Inti Illapa), rivers, valleys, mountan peaks, caves and plants. Any thing or place of a sacred nature was called a *huaca*.

Inca festivals as ancient rituals form the basis here of modern festivities celebrated in Catholic trappings. They celebrated the dry or rainy seasons. The planting of crops was honoured as was its growth as young corn. Rituals were performed to ensure the crops' well-being – The Great Ripening – and again notice was taken to wish well the harvest and its safe journey to market – Song of the Harvest.

During the dry winter months of July and August they celebrated the repair of terraces and irrigation canals and the assignment of *chacras* – Earthly Purification. The *chacras* or fields were intermittently made use of throughout the empire and were based on local populations. One year planted and five to eight years left fallow, the fields were thus rotated.

When the potatoes and other crops were planted the Incas performed the ceremony of Situa – Festival of the Queen, a purification in which all evils were expelled from the empire. In October there was a specal brewng of *chicha* for the Warachicuy feast in December, the initiation ceremony for young males. To make all this possible, the rains had to be nurtured like the land. If the rains were delayed, a *huacayllicuy*, or petition of rain, was held. All the llamas would be tied up without water so that their cries might cause the gods to send rain.

Christ has been identified with Inti Taita and the Virgin Mary with both Mama Quilla and Pacha Mama. The Virgin has been given Pacha Mama's role as patroness of agriculture, protector of crops and all living things. When the Indians called the Spanish guns Illapa they associated this with Inti Illapa (Father Thunder and Lightning), and he was associated with Saint James, the patron saint of Spain.

On the walls of a village called Chunchi was advertised a circus. That night I went to church. And then I went to the circus.

The church was a large building dominating the plaza. The townsfolk filed in and sat down. The altar, bathed in neon light, was plain. A priest filled the interior with a hum from his microphone and then asked everyone to repeat what he said. The church people mumbled something from memory. Several queued by the altar, waiting to be received, and one crippled youngster journeyed the length of the church to be touched. As the women kneeled, the men stood. The difficulty of Latin men subjugating themselves to higher authority was here obvious. And so the service ended. The priest asked everyone to embrace whoever was nearest and the congregation became twisted up with shaking hands. Merging into its final moments the organ became the iconic digestif.

Allowing the parishioners sufficient time to walk from the church to the big top, the ringmaster, scuffling his shoes in the sawdust, welcomed the town. Planked seats around the ring were sprung with bodies holding their breath. The fabulous Zolla was to perform in her sequins the most daring of acts on the trapeze. Pursed lips roared. Pocito the elephant wanted to dance on two legs, and strings of eyes widened in laughter. The clown besieged the audience to collaborate with his mock fiendish designs and a tent full of faces called out his name. Just then, in the mirth, I thought that there was a point in any journey when, among the people you have seen, the faces forgotten outnumber those remembered.

Each new face now takes on the guise of one already seen, like the wearing of a mask. Fit the mask, printed with familiar forms, and adjust it to fit to the face, and then you have never to meet a stranger. So the clown in his mask, a mask I find familiar, throws his bucket of clipped paper into a sea of completely unmemorable faces. Zolla disguised in sequins walked around the edge of the ring, blowing kisses from devil-red lips.

In two days I would be in Quito. I was a cock's-stride away from the equator. It was my turn to ride into that city in front of and behind all the rest who have ventured so far and risen and fell. I thought of Marco Polo talking to Kublai Khan.

Marco enters a city; he sees someone in a square living a life or an instant that could be his; he could now be in that man's place, if he had stopped in time, long ago; or if, long ago, at a crossroads, instead of taking one road he had taken the opposite one, and after long wondering he had come to be in the place of that man in that square. By now, from that real or hypothetical past of his, he is excluded; he cannot stop; he must go on to another city, where another of his pasts awaits him, or something perhaps that had been a possible future of his and is now someone else's present. Futures not achieved are only branches of the past: dead branches.

'Journeys to relive your past?' was the Khan's question at this point, a question which could also have been formulated: 'Journeys to recover your future?'

And Marco's answer was: 'Elsewhere is a negative mirror. The Traveller recognises the little that is his, discovering the much he has not had and will never have.'